Grace and Glory

KESWICK MINISTRY

Edited by David Porter

OM Publishing
PO Box 48, Bromley, Kent, England

Keswick Convention Council, England

Cover photo: The Rev. Canon K.W. Coates, BA
(Used by kind permission)

British Library Cataloguing in Publication Data

Grace and Glory: Keswick Ministry.
1. Bible—Critical studies
I. Porter, David *1945*–
220.6

ISBN 1-85078-100-1

OM Publishing is an imprint of Send The Light
(Operation Mobilisation),
PO Box 48, Bromley, Kent, England, BR1 3JH

Production and Printing in England by
Nuprint Ltd, Station Road, Harpenden, Herts, AL5 4SE.

CONTENTS

The Addresses

CHAIRMAN'S INTRODUCTION

Almost every year something new happens at Keswick. 1991 saw the first subtitle for the Convention. We decided on the theme of 'The kingdom, the power and the glory'. This seemed to fit very much with the expected Bible Readings and we were not disappointed. In no way did the subtitle theme take away from the long established sequence of teaching at Keswick. Indeed if anything that was more apparent this year than ever.

Two of our overseas speakers taking part for the first time gave their testimony to the value of Keswick ministry in their own spiritual development. R.T. Kendall and Luis Palau brought a very rich fare to the platform and it was quite moving to hear how the Lord had used Keswick preaching of the past to lead them into spiritual maturity. They were very aware of the sequence of teaching on the theme of holiness and their contributions helped to make a very memorable year of ministry.

1991 was marked by large crowds. There is no easy way to estimate the numbers at Keswick but it was generally accepted that this was the largest attendance for many years. Alongside such high numbers was a great spirit of worship and happy fellowship so that many Keswick regulars could speak of the warmest Convention they could remember, not in climatic terms but in spiritual.

There was a financial challenge brought to the thousands

attending, and the very wonderful response to this means that Keswick can look to the future with greater confidence. It is not out of keeping to stress the importance of giving in a Convention majoring on practical holiness. Indeed in the evangelical world of today this may be a message which needs to be heard as much as any other. In so many areas a lack of finance seems to be thwarting the work we believe God wants to be doing through His people.

This book will reveal something of the valuable teaching of Keswick 1991. As is often the case there was a lovely blend in the two sets of Bible Readings. Comparatively few people are present for both weeks and therefore this book can help to complement the ministry received at the Convention. R.T. Kendall's exposition of the life of Jacob made that somewhat controversial Old Testament figure very much alive and very contemporary. Roy Clements on the parables of the kingdom was uncomfortably challenging in his teaching. There was a freshness about this ministry which was very compelling. Those of us who were privileged to listen to both sets of Bible Readings knew that we had not only been at the feet of men of God but listening to the Lord Himself.

There was a power evident at Keswick in 1991, there was a sense of God's glory, and we believe that God's kingdom was forwarded. But through the printed page and the tape recording ministry it does not end there, and it is my prayer and conviction that the Word of God expounded at Keswick this year will go on spreading and multiplying.

Philip Hacking
Chairman of the Keswick Convention Council

EDITOR'S INTRODUCTION

The Keswick motto, 'All One in Christ Jesus', has a poignant ring in a year which has seen the final destruction of the Iron Curtain. Christians previously divided by impassable politics are today able to travel to countries they have longed to see for decades, and have fellowship with brothers and sisters they thought they would not meet this side of heaven. Though the great events of the Soviet revolution took place after Keswick 1991 had finished, Eastern Europe was much in the minds of Keswick participants this year, especially in view of the longstanding missionary commitment of the Convention.

But much remains ominously unsettled, as ancient ethnic tensions erupt in several European countries and some major long-term problems remain to be solved. And not just in Europe; many came to Keswick from parts of the world that are also turbulent and troubled.

It is a relevant backdrop to ministry that challenges its hearers to pursue practical personal holiness in a world that is firmly in the sovereign grasp of God. Editing the material has, as always, been a challenge and a blessing.

The material in this book has been edited and abridged to preserve as much of the flavour of the original event as possible and all the teaching. An interesting feature of the selection (made as usual by the Keswick Council) is that it reflects the way in which speakers who have not had the opportunity to prepare jointly find that God has blessed the platform ministry with remarkable unanimity and shared insights. We have included, in the addresses by Liam Goligher and David Cohen, both addresses from one of the shared two-message evening meetings.

Few of the speakers have had the chance to check the finished text, and it is important that readers appreciate that the book is a transcript of spoken addresses, not the revised and expanded versions that the speakers would have produced had book publication been their priority.

Bible quotations have been checked against the original, except where the speaker was clearly paraphrasing. Though the longer readings have often been cut, the full original references are always provided, so if you have a Bible to hand as you read your enjoyment and understanding will be much increased.

It is a pleasure to acknowledge the help of several free-lance typists who transcribed tapes on to word-processor disks.

For the addresses that were not included in this volume, and for the many excellent illustrations, anecdotes and jokes that had to be trimmed from the ones that were, the excellent Keswick tape and video library (details on p.219) is available.

David Porter

THE BIBLE READINGS

All's Well That Ends Well: Studies in the Life of Jacob

by Dr R. T. Kendall

1. Era of Deceit:
(Genesis 25:21–33:20)

There was a time when I identified most with Joseph; but the older I get, the more I identify with his father, Jacob. The older you get the more you can see the mistakes you have made, the more there is for you to feel guilty about. And Jacob provides a classic study in the problem of guilt.

Most Christians I know feel guilty about something. We don't admit it, because we can't admit it. Christians of all people aren't supposed to feel guilty. The truth is we feel guilty about feeling guilty. And so we deny that we feel guilty. The truth is, we need to come to terms with our feelings. This series of messages is designed to help anyone here who's wrestling with the problem of guilt.

Abraham was Paul's chief example of salvation by faith; Jacob, his chief example of salvation by grace. Faith is what we do, grace is what God does. Abraham's unworthy grandson Jacob was the world's greatest manipulator, the worst parent, the mama's boy, the schemer, the deceiver, the man who lost everything–or so he thought; the man who spent years and years feeling unthinkable guilt. And he was the world's greatest example of the sheer grace of God.

In Hebrews 11–the Westminster Abbey of the New Testament–Abraham is entitled to twelve verses, Moses gets seven, but Jacob gets only one. And what do you suppose that one verse says about him? Does it tell us about Jacob wrestling with God, about Jacob's ladder, about his name

being changed to Israel? Does it tell us that he was the
patriarchal father of the twelve tribes of Israel? Does it
mention Bethel, does it tell us about Leah and Rachel?

If you were writing chapter 11 of the Epistle to the
Hebrews, what would you have said about Jacob?

'By faith Jacob, when he was dying, blessed each of
Joseph's sons, and worshipped as he leaned on the top of his
staff' (11:21).

Why would the writer of this epistle select that obscure
event? There is even doubt precisely where it is to be found
in Genesis. But I venture to tell you that I think I know why
that event was chosen, and by the time this week is over we
will all see why Hebrews 11:21 tells it all.

The Barrenness

Our theme today is 'Era of Deceit'. It began with the barren
womb. 'Isaac prayed to the Lord on behalf of his wife,
because she was barren' (25:21). Though often regarded as a
curse, a barren womb was often a signal of great blessing to
come. Do you know what it is to be childless? Could it be
there's a couple here today who have prayed for years to have
a baby? You know the heartache, you know the hurt. Especially you ladies who are wanting to have a baby and are in
the company of mothers with two, three, four children and
sometimes of those who didn't even want to have children.
And how your heart aches!

Well, Rebekah was neither the first nor the last to have
her womb closed. From Sarah mother of Isaac, to Hannah
the mother of Samuel, to Elizabeth the mother of John the
Baptist, the barren womb was sometimes a symbol of promise in disguise. Sometimes the barrenness can be spiritual.
Sometimes God strategically closes the womb of the church,
awaiting a better day. Often people earmarked for unusual
mission have had their 'wombs' sovereignly closed. Sometimes God closes the womb of the church that He's going to
bless. When a church labours in prayer without blessing and
other churches seem to be filled to overflowing with blessing,
the Hannahs of this world weep tears of bitterness. Yet often,
I think, it is to demonstrate the promise of Isaiah: ' "Sing, O
barren woman, you who never bore a child; burst into song,

shout for joy, you who were never in labour; because more are the children of the desolate woman than of her who has a husband," says the Lord. "You will spread out to the right and to the left; your descendants will dispossess nations and settle in their desolate cities. Do not be afraid; you will not suffer shame. Do not fear disgrace; you will not be humiliated." ' (Isa. 54:1–4). Sometimes God strategically closes the womb because He's got plans that exceed our greatest expectations.

In this case it wasn't Rebekah but Isaac who prayed. Verse 21 says 'Isaac prayed to the Lord on behalf of his wife because she was barren' (verse 21). And yet he need not have worried. God's oath to Abraham was at stake. May I ask you, do you know what it is to have God swear an oath to you? Don't worry, His honour is at stake. Barrenness is often God's way of getting our attention, because when we are being blessed, when we are successful, we are often unteachable: we think we know everything. Yet when God allows even a spiritual barrenness to develop, it can be His way of driving us to our knees.

So Isaac prayed to the Lord on behalf of his wife. And perhaps you are here today wondering, why the unanswered prayer, why the delayed success?

I will never forget something Dr Lloyd-Jones said to me, almost as an aside: 'The worst thing that can happen to a man is to succeed before he is ready.' I wrote it down: I believe it's the greatest thing I ever heard him say. And it could be that the explanation for that unanswered prayer, that withheld sign that plagues you, is God's way of getting your attention; because in the meantime, you get to know Him in a way you had not before. Barrenness! See it as God's strategic sovereign act.

The Blueprint (25:22–23)

God was behind the barrenness; and He was also the architect of a carefully drawn blueprint. The barrenness is strategic, the blueprint surprising. His plan often breaks traditional patterns. 'The older will serve the younger.' The firstborn by natural right was to inherit double what other children would inherit, and that was God's idea. But God isn't in a theological straight-jacket. God is sovereign.

He later said to Moses 'I will have mercy on whom I will have mercy and will be gracious to whom I will be gracious.' It reminds us that those born to us are not ours but God's. God alone gives life. And He retains the prerogative to do with every person what He wills, so that Paul quotes Malachi to the Romans: 'Jacob I loved, but Esau I hated' (Rom. 9:13).

Don't ask me to explain that! I only know that Paul didn't mind saying earlier 'Yet, before the twins were born or had done anything good or bad–in order that God's purpose in election might stand: not by works but by him who calls–she was told, "The older will serve the younger" ' (Rom. 9:11).

The blueprint was drawn up by God Himself. ' "For my thoughts are not your thoughts, neither are your ways my ways" declares the Lord. "As the heavens are higher than the earth, so are my ways higher than your ways and my thoughts than your thoughts" ' (Isa. 55:8–9).

This blueprint wasn't Isaac's idea. It wasn't Rebekah's idea. Jacob didn't know about it. But there was to be an anointing on Jacob. It was an unconscious anointing. He would later say 'God was in this place and I knew it not.' He would one day worship, leaning on the top of his staff, in amazement that there was an anointing on him all along. It is often best that we can't see the hand of God on us, blessing others. Most of us couldn't handle the truth; Moses didn't know his face was shining.

And so God had His finger on Jacob while still in his mother's womb. It makes us think of Psalm 139, a psalm very relevant for the present time: 'You created my inmost being; you knit me together in my mother's womb...My frame was not hidden from you when I was made in the secret place...' (Psa. 139:13–16).

Life is special from the moment of conception. God had His hand on Jacob while still in his mother's womb. This didn't mean that Jacob would be perfect. That is what is so encouraging! Don't tell me that I have to be perfect in order to be used by God. Jacob was a demonstration of overruling grace, not because he did everything right. 'We have this treasure in earthen vessels that the excellency of the power may be of God, and not of us' (2 Cor. 4:7). God sees the end from the beginning.

The Birth (25:24–26)

The prophetic word to Rebekah was proved right. Twin boys were born. Thus the promise to Abraham was being carried out. And yet the line was to be through Isaac, not Ishmael, and further carried on through Jacob, not Esau. There was a promise for Ishmael and a promise for Esau, and they also carried out the oath to Abraham and Isaac. But God had special plans for Jacob.

Yet God calls each of us in such a manner that we can never boast. 'Who makes you different from anyone else? What do you have that you did not receive? And if you did receive it, why do you boast as though you did not?' (1 Cor. 4:7).

And Jacob leaning on the top of his staff would know that there was no way he could take the slightest credit for Joseph becoming prime minister of Egypt; that was out of his hands, and he had a thousand reasons to be ashamed. So he knew that at the bottom of it all was the sheer grace of God.

Names–especially in the Old Testament–have significance. They named Esau 'red', for his colour. The name Jacob means 'he grasps the heel'. Figuratively, it means 'he deceives'. Today we might call someone a 'heel'. But never forget, God loves to take the 'heels' of this world, those whom we would reject, and turn them into trophies. Jesus said 'I have not come to call the righteous but sinners to repentance.' And He said to the priests and elders, 'I tell you the truth, the tax collectors and prostitutes are entering the kingdom of God ahead of you' (Matt. 21:31).

God loves to call the Matthews and Zacchaeuses of this world. He continues to use instruments that often seem repugnant to us. Over the years I've watched those whom God would put His finger on, and I have often felt betrayed. How dare God use a person like that! Yet the next time you criticise a man who doesn't fit your traditional mould, just remember Jacob; just remember the Lord Jesus Christ, who

was called 'the stone which was set at nought by you builders,
which is become the head of the corner' (Acts 4:11 AV).

The Birthright (25:27–34)

The two boys were opposites (verses 27–28). Esau was a man
after Isaac's heart. You could call him a man's man. He was a
skilful hunter. Jacob was the homebody, the 'mama's boy' if
there ever was one, rather like John Wesley who was Susan-
nah's favourite son. Often children under the same roof will
be opposites. If one is good at sport, the other will be good at
books. It is perhaps God's way of making us competitive.
Esau was the outdoor man but Jacob was the cleverer.

You see, Jacob grew up being told he was the baby. Esau
was only seconds older but Jacob was still the baby. And he
knew what that meant. It meant that he got half of what Esau
would inherit; and Esau would inherit their father's blessing,
which was what really mattered.

It is unprofitable to speculate whether Rebekah ever told
Jacob of the prophetic word from God that preceded his
birth, 'the older shall serve the younger'. For all I know Jacob
knew about it for years. One day Esau came in famished.
Jacob, the homebody who had learned to cook like his
mother and knew how to make it smell so good, had just
fixed a stew, perfectly timed. Verse 30, 'Esau...said to
Jacob, "Quick, let me have some of that red stew! I'm
famished!" '

It was a reasonable request. But suddenly Jacob the
manipulator elevated the conversation to an eternal level.
Right out of the blue he said, 'First sell me your birthright.'
What an impertinent, unfair thing to say! But Jacob wasn't
joking. Once Esau realised his brother was serious he began
to rationalise. 'Well, I'm going to die. If I do, my birthright
will be worthless. If I eat at least I'll be alive.' And so Esau
was 'godless' (Heb. 12:16). Instead of living for eternal princi-
ples, he lived for the here-and-now, and he did a stupid thing;
he sold his birthright. Esau could never blame God for what
he did. Esau had only himself to blame.

We can derive a double principle from this story: that
when it comes to God's purpose in the gospel, if we are

saved, it is by grace alone. And if we are disinherited it is by our own choice.

The Blessing (27:1–40)

We now move to chapter 27. Apparently old Isaac had not heard that Esau had sold his birthright. In a sense, what Esau did would prove nothing, because what really mattered was Isaac's patriarchal blessing. If Esau got the blessing of the firstborn, even though he had sold his birthright, that transaction would have been meaningless. What mattered then was not the stolen birthright but the one on whom the blessing came. Esau had no intention of telling his father what he had done. He should have; he had sworn an oath. The honourable act would have been to go to his father and say 'This is what I've done.'

He might have been sorry, he might have wept, but he should have come clean. But he was too ashamed to do it. Breaking the oath, then and now, is the worst kind of dishonesty. The only advantage of the birthright then was that it guaranteed the blessing, which was what ultimately mattered.

Old and feeble, Isaac ordered Esau to kill some wild game, prepare it and get his blessing. Esau wasn't telling the old man anything. He headed for the open country. He appeared to have escaped from his former folly. Getting the patriarchal blessing meant more to Esau than integrity.

Enter Rebekah, who overheard the whole conversation. What follows is more than I can understand. Jacob the manipulator was trained by a manipulative mother. 'God moves in a mysterious way His wonders to perform.' Rebekah was determined that Esau's oath to Jacob should be honoured, no matter how. She prepared the meal. Jacob covered his hands and neck with goat skins, so it would appear to the blind father that he was Esau. It worked. The blind father felt his son and concluded it was Esau.

Isaac gave Jacob his blessing. And it turned out to be Isaac's finest hour. It is what earned Isaac a place in Hebrews chapter 11, because Hebrews 11:20 says 'By faith Isaac blessed Jacob and Esau in regard to their future.' Even having been tricked, Isaac–who had been a weak man, perhaps the most lack-lustre figure in the Old Testament–was in this moment

strong. 'I have blessed Jacob and he will be blessed.' He did
his best to give Esau a blessing.

Esau tried to get Isaac to change his mind, but it was too
late. We're told he could find no place of repentance though
he sought it with tears. And Esau was now filled with bitterness.

The Burden (27:41–45)

Jacob got the blessing, but a burden came with it. It was truly
a mixed blessing. Jacob now carried with him the burden of
Esau who now lived for one thing and one thing alone:
revenge. 'Your brother Esau is consoling himself with the
thought of killing you' (27:42).

Jacob succeeded in getting what he wanted most in all the
world, the patriarchal blessing. But do you suppose that he
was allowed to enjoy it? No. An era of dread and terror was
now Jacob's. It made him a man on the run, a hunted man.

We may wish there were nothing but unmixed blessings in
this life, but how often it is true: when you get what you want
you also get what you don't want. And Jacob got what he
wanted but he wasn't able to enjoy it. He lived in perpetual
fear. A gifted person always has the thorn in the flesh. Paul
prayed three times that his would go, and all God would say
was, 'My grace is sufficient for you, for my power is made
perfect in weakness' (2 Cor. 12:9). Anointing is paralleled by
suffering. Some of you are in retirement and you know that
feeling. Revival always carries the unwanted excesses. Roses
always have their thorns. We wish there were such a thing as
an unmixed blessing.

Jacob couldn't fully enjoy the blessing he so eagerly
wanted. He couldn't even be at home. And you know the
feeling of having God put you in a place where strategically
you belong, because that's where you will work for Him and
not be diverted by other things? Perhaps you know the pain
of not getting to be where you'd like to be. Jacob had what he
wanted but he couldn't enjoy it.

Some years ago I remember saying goodbye to my friend
Bruce Porter, who at the time was pastor of the Island
Community Church in the Florida Keys, the spot that I love
most in all the world.

I said to Bruce, 'You lucky man, to live here!' And he replied, 'I'd rather be in North Carolina.'

The next day I said to O.S. Hawkins, my friend in Fort Lauderdale, 'You lucky man, to live here!' And he replied, 'I'd rather be in Texas.'

And it hit me: here were two men God was sovereignly using, and they couldn't be where they wanted to be.

I know, in my heart of hearts, that if I got to live in the Florida Keys I would rot. I would do nothing but lie out in the sun and fish. So God has put me in a place where the weather won't allow that! He has a way of removing what stops us looking beyond, lest we enjoy things around us too much.

Jacob couldn't be at home; he lived in fear of his life. God ordered it that way. We all are in danger of loving this world too much. That's why God has made heaven. Do you want to know why it is that you get older and older and the tears continue to flow, and you look for that moment when you are free from some kind of worry or pain? God wants you to look forward to heaven, that place where He will wipe away all tears. There'll be no more death, no crying or pain. For the former things will have passed away.

Jacob had a burden, and that is what prepared him for Bethel, the place of his holiest moment. He went from the blessing, to the burden, to Bethel. And God wants to lead all of us to Bethel, as we shall see tomorrow.

The Bridle (29:16–30)

We move now to chapter 29, where the bridle enters Jacob's life. That is what Laban turned out to be, a bridle around his neck. At long last, Jacob the manipulator was to meet his match. God has a curious way of letting us face ourselves in others. That which so often makes you so angry with another person is really something that is really prominent in yourself.

I'll never forget being on my way to Westminster Chapel once when we were living in Ealing. We were approaching Marble Arch and the driver ahead of me was going really slowly. I began to honk my horn and shake my fist. Finally I overtook him. But do you know, I began to get interested in something on the car radio, and soon I slowed down in my turn, and soon that same person was honking at me. And I thought, Isn't that something? It taught me a lesson.

Jacob met his match. Laban, Rebekah's brother, had a beautiful daughter, Rachel. Jacob actually met Rachel before he met Laban, and when he laid eyes on her it was love at first sight. He was so overcome that all he could do was stand and weep. It's one of the most beautiful love stories in the Bible. After meeting Laban he promised to work for him for seven years if he could have Rachel for his wife. And so Laban said, 'You have a deal.'

'So Jacob served seven years to get Rachel, but they seemed like only a few days to him because of his love for her. Then Jacob said to Laban, "Give me my wife. My time is completed, and I want to lie with her." ' The wedding and honeymoon were all in order and everything seemed to be going to plan. But then, 'when evening came, [Laban] took his daughter Leah'—who wasn't exactly the beauty queen of the day—'and gave her to Jacob, and Jacob lay with her.' The next morning Jacob realised he had slept with Leah, the least desirable of Laban's daughters. 'What is this you have done to me? I served you for Rachel, didn't I? Why have you deceived me?' (29:25).

Talk about the pot calling the kettle black! But Laban made excuse: 'Oh, Jacob, sorry—I forgot to tell you. It's not our custom here to give the younger daughter in marriage before the older one.' And so in this era of deceit Jacob was now forced to work another seven years for Rachel. Jacob had deceived Esau and Isaac. Laban had deceived Jacob. But this bridle around Jacob's neck for fourteen years would result in the world being blessed.

And the lesson for us from this is that those were fourteen difficult years for Jacob. He wasn't exactly blessed, and he didn't appreciate what was going on. And yet those fourteen years could be called the most under-estimated era in the life of Jacob. They weren't doing a lot for Jacob, but they were going to do a lot for the world.

Jacob never really appreciated Leah. She was unwanted and unattractive, but it was Leah, not Rachel, who gave him six of his twelve sons including Levi and Judah. Rachel's womb after he got her was closed like Rebekah's, but even when she gave birth to Joseph and Benjamin, it has to be said that the blessing of the future of Israel and the church did not come through Rachel's sons. It was through the wife he did not want, the consequence of Laban putting this bridle on Jacob, that Israel's greater sons came, including Judah, through whom the Lord Jesus Christ came. It was through Leah that the world was really blessed.

And I say all that because what you have regarded as a bridle involuntarily imposed on you may in fact be the means of the greatest blessing to others. One day you will be most thankful for that time and see it as your finest era. I don't think Jacob ever appreciated Leah, but without her there would be no twelve sons of Israel, no Levi to give rise to the priesthood, no Judah through whom the Lord Jesus Christ was to come.

Perhaps you haven't appreciated your wife or your husband. Perhaps you haven't appreciated your church, your job, your children. Perhaps you haven't appreciated that person who has been thrust upon you. Be not forgetful to entertain strangers; some entertain angels unaware.

But what God is maybe doing through some of you right now, in this era of the bridle that seems so hard, may mean that you're not being blessed – but the world is. And one day you will see it.

The Breakthrough (33:4–20)

All these years Jacob lived with an impediment, called fear. It was one thing to be stuck under Laban's thumb, but at least he was safe from Esau. But fear of Esau was not gone.

I doubt that a day went by in which any stranger, any group of travellers seen in the distance failed to strike terror into Jacob. 'Here he comes! This is it! It's all going to end today...' It was only a matter of time, Jacob knew it. Esau would find him. He was still a hunted man. Fear is the greatest bridle in the world. It paralyses, it deceives. But 'God hath not given us the spirit of fear; but of power, and of love, and of a sound mind' (2 Tim. 1:7 AV).

All this time Jacob was oppressed, fearing Esau, and one day it happened: 'There was Esau, coming with his four hundred men; so he divided the children among Leah, Rachel and the two maidservants' (33:1).

Jacob lived in dread for fourteen years. By the way, what are you afraid of? Have you come to Keswick with a heavy heart? What is it you're dreading, what bad thing are you so sure is going to happen?

I remember some years ago having one of the greatest trials I've ever had in my life; I lived in continual fear. One day I came across a simple little verse. 'Who is going to harm you if you are eager to do good?' (1 Pet. 3:13).

What are you so sure is going to happen?

Ye fearful saints fresh courage take,
The clouds ye so much dread
Are big with mercy, and shall break
In blessings on your head.

(William Cowper)

Lo and behold–'He himself went on ahead and bowed down to the ground seven times as he approached his brother. But'– would you believe it?–'Esau ran to meet Jacob and embraced him; he threw his arms around his neck and kissed him. And they wept. Esau looked up and saw the women and children. "Who are these with you?" he asked. Jacob answered, "They are the children God has graciously given your servant." '

Jacob can hardly believe what is happening.

There are two ways in which fears are dissolved. One is when your external situation changes, the other is when you have an internal victory, such as Paul describes: 'Do not be anxious about anything . . . and the peace of God, which transcends all understanding, will guard your hearts and your minds in Christ Jesus' (Phil. 4:6–7).

Jacob could hardly believe what was happening. Verse 8: 'Esau asked "What do you mean by all these droves I met?"

"To find favour in your eyes, my lord," he said.

But Esau said, "I already have plenty, my brother. Keep what you have for yourself."

"No, please!" said Jacob. "If I have found favour in your eyes, accept this gift from me. For to see your face is like seeing the face of God, now that you have received me favourably." '

They parted best of friends. It may surprise you that today's enemy could be tomorrow's friend. Watch what you say about your enemy in the meantime, then you won't have so much to blush about when you make up! Remember that that enemy is a frail person and wants to need you. And know that there's no fear in love. The things we dread are almost never as bad as we think they're going to be. There was a time when it seemed impossible that Jacob and Esau could ever meet like that.

> Judge not the Lord by feeble sense
> But trust Him for His grace;
> Behind a frowning providence,
> He hides a smiling face.
>
> His purposes will ripen fast,
> Unfolding every hour;
> The bud may have a bitter taste,
> But sweet will be the flower.

(William Cowper)

2. Era of Dreams
(Genesis 28:1–35:15)

Can you remember that era of your dreams, when you were virtually at the beginning of life, beginning to ask: 'What will I do with my life, who will I marry, will I achieve my goals?'

Where there is no vision the people perish. I grew up hearing the maxim 'Hitch your wagon to a star'. Think big! I was taught that ambition is not a bad word. Martin Luther used to say, 'God uses sex to drive a man to marriage, ambition to drive a man to service, fear to drive a man to faith.' Before I felt the call to preach I wanted to be a barrister. And every American boy dreams of being President. I can't honestly tell you I've given up that hope– President Kendall!–though I must say it's looking less and less likely…

In ancient times ambition was set by patriarchal blessing. That is why Jacob wanted Isaac's valedictory blessing. It was what gave him scope for ambition. That is why Esau tried to get his father Isaac to change his mind. Esau got a blessing, but its scope was narrow. What Jacob got meant the sky was the limit, for the patriarchal blessing told Jacob how ambitious he could be. Esau knew he could never move beyond Isaac's word. Jacob knew he could dream the impossible dream realistically.

The Valedictory Blessing (28:1–5)

In fact Isaac gave Jacob two valedictory blessings. The first you will find in Genesis 27:27–29: 'May God give you of heaven's dew and of earth's richness—an abundance of grain and new wine. May nations serve you and peoples bow down to you. Be lord over your brothers, and may the sons of your mother bow down to you. May those who curse you be cursed and those who bless you be blessed.'

The patriarchal blessing was the equivalent of the oath. It was unconditional, absolute, irrevocable. Many Old Testament promises are given with certain conditions, but this was the oath level. Jacob therefore had a lot going for him. He was promised prosperity: 'May God give you of heaven's dew...' He was given the prerogative of the first-born: 'May nations serve you and peoples bow down to you. Be lord over your brothers...', and he was given *carte blanche* protection: 'May those who curse you be cursed and those who bless you be blessed.'

But the second blessing comes in 28:3–4. There was the promise of a large family—and there was the blessing of Abraham. Nothing was greater than that. 'May He give you and your descendants the blessing given to Abraham, so that you may take possession of the land where you now live as an alien, the land God gave to Abraham.'

So what was given by oath to Abraham was passed on to Jacob. The land would be his. With such a patriarchal blessing the world was in his pocket. Nobody who ever lived had more to look forward to. His wildest dream would not exceed Isaac's scope. Moreover, there was no way it couldn't happen.

And yet there came a time when Jacob needed to know for sure that what Isaac was saying really was from God. I asked yesterday, I ask again today: did you ever have God swear an oath to you? Are you aware that the Epistle to the Hebrews was written partly to encourage discouraged Christians to believe that God was willing to swear an oath to them? According to Hebrews 6:18 there are 'two unchangeable things' (the AV says 'two immutable things'). Do you know what the two are? The promise and the oath.

What's the difference? Well, they are both equally true,

but it's easier to believe the oath. Sometimes God accommodates us in our weakness and swears an oath to us and we're never quite the same again. Let me illustrate. God gave a promise to Abraham, Jacob's grandfather: 'Count the stars. So shall your seed be.' And we are told that Abraham believed it. It became Paul's foundation for justification by faith alone–'Abraham believed God, and it was credited to him as righteousness' (Rom. 4:3). But it seems that after a while Abraham himself became discouraged. Nothing was happening, Sarah was getting older, he had no children; and he began to say, 'Lord, did I really hear you correctly?' And God would reappear and give Abraham another promise.

It's rather like when you go to church week after week, and you say 'Lord, I really need you to speak to me today.' And God does. And it's the same old promise. You can read from Genesis 12 to 22 and see eight or nine times that God accommodated Abraham, but only at the promise level. It was just enough to encourage him and to keep him going a while longer.

But one day God swore an oath to Abraham. It was the occasion when he became willing to sacrifice Isaac. And God said, 'Now I know you really love me.' And we read in Hebrews 6:13–14, 'When God made his promise to Abraham, since there was no-one greater for him to swear by, he swore by himself, saying, "I will surely bless you and give you many descendants." '

That was God speaking at the oath level. The oath is God's accommodation to our weakness. It is also called God's 'rest'. Hebrews 4:9–10: 'There remaineth therefore a rest to the people of God. For he that has entered into his rest...hath ceased from his own works, as God did from his.' It's when you come to rest in God and He is so real to you.

You wonder, how might this oath be ours in the Christian life? In many ways. It may be assurance of eternal salvation: God can swear an oath to you: you are saved. It is as though you already have one foot in heaven, even though you have many years to live. You know you are saved. Or it may be assurance of answered prayer. I could go on and on.

God can swear an oath to you. He still grants us the oath today. The wonder of it is, it sets you free and it gives you so much to live for; and that is what Jacob needed. So it wasn't enough to just have the valedictory. Could he believe that the patriarchal blessing would be owned of God?

The Vision (28:10–12)

For the first time Jacob was beginning to discover God for himself. Up until now his hope was based upon Isaac's word, because that patriarchal blessing was the most coveted thing in the world. Yet in a sense it was the word of man. Could he be sure that this word would come to pass? How could he know for sure all these things would really happen? There was only one thing certain. Only God could make it happen.

The patriarchal blessing was one thing; whether God in heaven really was behind it was another. After all, Jacob never forgot that he had stolen the birthright and deceived his father to get the blessing. Yes, Isaac did say, 'It's too late for you Esau, Jacob will be blessed.' But then Jacob began to wonder, what does God say? What if God in heaven disapproved? Isaac's blessing was one thing, perhaps God's blessing was something else.

Jacob had what Daniel would call 'a night vision'. It happened when he was asleep, yes. But it was clearly a vision. Most of us know it as 'Jacob's ladder', but Jacob actually saw two things. A stairway reaching from earth to heaven, and angels walking up and down on the ladder. This was the most wonderful thing yet to happen to Jacob. God Himself was in direct communication with Jacob. Up until now the blessing was, as it were, second-hand. But now God Himself had directly stepped into his life.

It reminds me of the effect Jesus had upon the woman of Samaria (John 4). She went into the town and called her neighbours who invited Jesus to stay with them. Then 'they said to the woman, "We no longer believe just because of what you said; now we have heard for ourselves, and we know that this man really is the Saviour of the world" ' (John 4:42).

Jacob needed to know for himself that the sovereign God of heaven and earth was behind the patriarchal blessing. May I ask you, have you discovered God for yourself? Perhaps like me you were brought up in a Christian home. But there came a time when you needed to know that there is a God in the heavens—you had to see Him, you had to feel Him. Have you come to that place? Perhaps you've heard great preaching over the years, you've read the biographies of the great saints. But have you personally met the God of those people? Have you met the God of Jonathan Edwards, Charles Spurgeon, Hudson Taylor? Have you come to know personally the God of Abraham, Isaac and Jacob?

This vision meant three things.

First, access to God, the greatest access in the world. Second, the promise of dialogue with God; now Jacob had been given the promise that he could talk to God and God would talk to him. Third, most wonderful of all, the approval of God. For Jacob knew for himself all that Isaac promised was true; and all that Isaac promised was owned by God Himself. To have this heavenly confirmation was rest of soul. Jacob could now cease from his striving and his anxiety.

The Voice (28:13–15)

There above him, or beside him, stood the Lord. It does not say he saw the Lord directly. No man has seen God at any time. 'No-one may see me and live,' said God to Moses (Ex. 33:20). But Jacob knew that the Lord was there. There was no doubt he was having an immediate confrontation with God. But the point I want to make is this: the vision gave way to the voice. The vision would have proved almost nothing, or meaningless, without it. God was speaking.

'Thou hast magnified thy word above all thy name' (Psa. 138:2 AV). God's 'word' refers to God's integrity, His 'name' refers to His reputation and His power. You see, God is more interested in His own integrity than in His reputation. People say, 'Why does God allow this to happen? Don't you know that God is getting a bad reputation when He allows war or poverty or suffering?' But God can handle His reputation. The one thing that matters to Him pre-eminently is His word, His own integrity. That is the heartbeat of God. The vision gave way to the voice.

Many today are interested today in signs and wonders, in the gifts of the Spirit, in seeing God work powerfully; and I don't blame them. But I have to tell you it is no certain sign of how spiritual you are that you desire things like that. Even King Herod desired to see Jesus because he wanted to see Him do a miracle. And there's a natural instinct in all of us to want to see the unusual. But God cares most for His word. Even on Easter Sunday morning, nobody actually saw Jesus raised from the dead. They arrived too late. But we read, 'Then they remembered his words' (Luke 24:8). The vision gave way to the voice.

And the voice is what explicitly confirmed Isaac's valedictory blessing. The voice of God said, 'Here is what I will do.' Let me call your attention to something that will be important later: the end of 28:15, where God says 'I will not leave you until I have done what I promised you,' having just said, 'I will bring you back to this land.' That must have given him pause. How could a word like that come? Perhaps some of you have had a particular word from God and you think, 'I don't see how this can happen.' But there will come a time when the scripture that you didn't understand, or that word given to you, all falls into place. The vision meant that God was at work. It was the voice however that put the seal on what God was going to do.

The Vow (28:16–20)

I am fascinated by this. He realised on reflection that God had been at work. Have you done this? Many of us appreciate the good old days too late. Looking back on a moment that you didn't appreciate at the time, you begin to see that God was at work then. And you realise, 'Mmm–that was God! If only I had absorbed it then.'

I think there are two kinds of revival. One is when God pours out His spirit in an unmistakeable way. But there are also revivals in which God is at work but some people lack discernment to see it. Jacob had underestimated the 'certain place' of verse 11: he would thereafter see it as a hallowed place.

Perhaps you've had an experience with the Lord that you didn't appreciate at the time. The lesson we learn is that we could have had our eyes open sooner. And our lesson for today is that we could have our eyes opened now. Jesus said to the disciples, 'You can discern the face of the sky—but why can't you discern the signs of the times?' (see Luke 12:56).

Jonathan Edwards taught us that the task of every generation is to discover in which direction the sovereign redeemer is moving, then move in that direction. It is a wonderful thing if we can see, at the time, that God is at work. So Jacob says, "Surely the LORD is in this place, and I was not aware of it." And he was afraid and said, "How awesome is this place! This is none other than the house of God, this is the gate of heaven." '

The sooner we can come to this the better. I sometimes wonder if a definition of spirituality would be, 'Closing the time gap between moment and memory'. In other words, how long does it take you to admit this was God at work? For some it takes years, for some months, for some weeks, days, hours, seconds...and narrowing the time gap between the moment and the memory would help you to refine your spiritual sensitivity and avoid the delayed reaction: 'I wish I'd been aware of what God was doing.'

Jacob named that certain place Bethel (verse 19). Never mind what it used to be called, from now on that place was Bethel. Do you have your Bethel? For some of you this week will be your Bethel.

> O God of Bethel! by Whose hand
> Thy people still are fed;
> Who through this weary pilgrimage
> Hast all our fathers led.
>
> (Philip Doddridge and Michael Bruce)

Bethel became a precious symbol. In subsequent history it meant so much to Jacob. It wasn't merely something sentimental, it meant everything to him. And he wanted to commemorate Bethel. How can we commemorate our Bethel? Jacob set up a pillar and poured oil on top of it. He renamed the place and made a twofold vow: one, that the Lord would be his God, and second—are you ready for this?—he became a tither.

John Wesley said the last thing to get converted is our pocket-book. You see, tithing is not a Mosaic intervention. It was a patriarchal commitment. You want to know how you can show your gratitude to God? You give; you prove how much God really does mean to you. And some of you have never learned the joy of giving God His one-tenth, and the happy discovery, the mathematical incredulity that God can make the ninety percent you keep for yourself go as far as the hundred percent you started out with–my Dad used to say the ninety percent goes *further* than the hundred percent.

What a wonderful thing if this year we could go into next year in the black! Some of us need to do just that. That is what Jacob did to show his gratitude.

The Visitors (32:1–2)

Everything we have just examined preceded Jacob's time with Laban. He thereafter met his Leah and Rachel. He saw the beginnings of God's wonderful promise. You will recall how Jacob dreaded meeting Esau, but he need not have worried. He was affirmed by his special visitors. He should have realised then that God was up to something. But these visitors came as Jacob was still in that dread and terror of running into Esau. And so these special visitors came. They were angels. In his vision he had seen angels walking up and down the ladder. Now angels met him on his way to meet Esau, and it was no vision.

Most of us have never seen an angel. But remember 'Do not forget to entertain strangers, for by so doing some people have entertained angels without knowing it' (Heb. 13.2). This place may be filled with angels, if we could only see with our spiritual eyes. 'The angel of the Lord encamps around those who fear him, and he delivers them' (Psa. 34:7). I think that's why they like Keswick–they can all get together when we get together! Psalm 91:11 tells us 'For he will command his angels concerning you to guard you in all your ways.' Do you know that psalm was the most popular psalm among Christians in the air-raid shelters during the 1940s blitz?

As Christians we can't lose. We have the Holy Spirit, we have angels. Angels do what God tells them to do, and He will command His angels concerning you.

The Victory (32:22–32)

Before Jacob was to have a victory over Esau, God knew he needed something that was far greater: a victory over himself. He wanted an external victory, but God knew he needed an internal one.

Some of you are afraid of the future for various reasons, and you just want the situation to change externally, then you'll be happy. But there's a greater victory, and that is when something internal happens to you.

That is what God wanted to do for Jacob, because when we get the victory from within, we can face a thousand worlds. So many of us only know the victory from outside, when the situation that threatens us is removed and the problem that worried us goes away. But God wanted Jacob to get a taste of victory from within and in advance. What we are going to see now was to be probably the highest watermark in his life so far. And it all happened because of his dread of Esau.

God uses our greatest fears to change us within, and to get our attention. The stress and turmoil over Esau led to what was probably Jacob's sweetest victory. Jacob's problem was that he had succcumbed to a defence mechanism called 'projection'. We've all done it. We let our fears take over, especially if we are not right in ourselves. We look at some person we know and say, 'Oh, you're angry with me today. You were right next to me and you didn't speak to me.' And the person replies, 'Oh I'm sorry–I didn't even see you.' But we thought they did, we projected. We've all done this, believing our suspicions without knowing the facts.

Well, Jacob knew that Esau was out to get him. It wasn't quite paranoia; after all, he had reason to fear the worst, and he was prepared for it. His plan was to pacify Esau with gifts. But God said, 'Jacob, there's something better for you. You need to realise you've got more serious problems: not what Esau thinks of you, but what I think of you.' Jacob needed to realise that this was his fundamental problem. Our most serious problems are not with people but with God. We need to realise that if we are going to go forward, we must do it by getting God's attention, as Isaiah 58:1–3 describes.

We need to realise that we must have God's attention and

that He must show His approval of us. This was the lesson Jacob was to learn. And it all began in a lack-lustre place in the middle of the night. It was to be a night of nights! Who has despised the day of small things? Who has despised the place of small things? Who has despised the night of small things?

Jacob suddenly found himself in a wrestling match. We are only told that he was wrestling with a man; Jacob began the match thinking that the man was an enemy. But by daybreak he had somehow recognised him as a friend. Martin Luther said that you must know God as an enemy before you can know Him as a friend. And not only was this man a friend; Jacob could see that here was a friend with authority and power.

Jacob overcame the man, who begged to be released. 'Never in a thousand years!' said Jacob. 'I will not let you go unless you bless me.' For he discerned that this man had infinite authority. The man's blessing could now change everything, and it was to be the best thing that happened to him yet. And what is so encouraging is that as Jacob got older he was having one experience with God after the other, and each was better.

The man no doubt was an angel. Jacob had the upper hand and the angel was pinned down. He saw his chance and took full advantage of it. Why? Because he wanted power with God. That is what we should want more than anything in the world. Jacob said, 'I am not going to let you go until you bless me.' The Welsh revival of 1904 started because Evan Roberts locked the doors and said 'We are not going out until God comes down.'

'What is your name?' the angel asked.

'Jacob.'

Then came a reply that would change everything. It would change history, it would mean a new identity for Jacob, for his family, for a nation: 'Your name will no longer be Jacob, but Israel, because you have struggled with God and with men and have overcome.' The Authorised Version says, 'You have power with God'.

I'd rather have that than anything. It is what is needed today more than anything. It seems to me that our problem today is that we are in a wrestling match with each other. We write our books and articles saying who is wrong, and in the meantime the world is going to hell and the devil laughs. I call on all of us today to enter into a wrestling match with God. Let's not be particular how unspectacular the place or how uneventful the time. The time is now–not next week, not tomorrow. We need to get God's attention and recognise our need for anointing, so that we might receive the honour that comes from God only.

Jesus said, 'How can you believe, which receive honour one of another, and seek not the honour that cometh from God only?' (John 5:44 AV). Jacob could see he was on the brink of having that and he wasn't going to let that angel go. We are told that Jacob called the place Peniel, 'because I saw God face to face, and yet my life was spared'. And as he passed Peniel, 'he was limping because of his hip'. I warn you, a wrestling match with God will leave you injured. The impediment of fear that characterised his dread of Esau was to go, but God put another in its place, for there will always be a thorn in the flesh for the one who puts God first.

The Virtue (35:1–7)

Jacob has become a grandfather. Many years have passed. The dread of Esau was now a distant memory; he had a new kind of problem. It's inevitable for all of us, I suppose. His troubles were now domestic. In Genesis 34 you have the sad story of Dinah and the Shechemites. We don't have time to go into that, but it was an awful problem and a heart-ache for Jacob. And he had a quarrel with Simeon and Levi: 'You have brought trouble on me by making me a stench to the Canaanites and Perizzites, the people living in this land' (34:30).

Something has happened that can only be called grieving the Spirit. Jacob became bitter. He's having a new kind of problem, and having to show that he can be a man and learn not to grieve the Holy Spirit even close at home. He's in confusion. The visions, the voice–what was happening now? God said 'Go up to Bethel.' Jacob needed a revival in his soul.

There's nothing like domestic trouble to drive you to your

knees. Perhaps some of you today are wearing a mask. Your marriages are on the rocks, you're hurting and no one knows the nightmare at home. But this can be God's way of getting your attention.

Jacob needed a fresh touch from God. There was a place for this; it was called Bethel. Is God calling you back to Bethel? Are you like those described in Revelation 2:4–5: you've lost your first love, you need to repent and do what you did first? Can I ask you: how much do you read your Bible? How much do you actually pray? How much time do you actually spend alone with God in prayer?

Go back to Bethel.

The road to Bethel was paved with re-consecration. What a pity that foreign gods had crept in (verse 2)! No wonder there was so much internal trouble. Jacob knew it. 'Get rid of the foreign gods you have with you, and purify yourselves and change your clothes' And to the everlasting credit of his sons, they all went with him.

What do you do when you grieve the Holy Spirit? You surrender two things: peace and presence of mind. The scary thing about grieving the Holy Spirit is that we almost never realise we're doing it at the time. We find out later that's what we did. When Samson gave his secret to Delilah he didn't feel a thing: 'He did not know that the Lord had left him' (Judg. 16:20). He found out: when he tried to do the same old thing, he didn't have the power of God. And when we grieve the Spirit there is confusion and a weakness.

We're called to grace and virtue (2 Peter 1:3). Add to your faith virtue which is goodness. And how do you know if you've lost virtue? When you lose two things: peace and presence of mind. But they were getting it right, on their way to Bethel. And a wonderful fringe benefit emerged, that comes to the church when the church gets right with God: 'Then they set out, and the terror of God fell upon the towns all around them so that no-one pursued them' (verse 5).

It reminds me of the power that was in the earliest church after Ananias and Sapphira were struck dead by the Holy Spirit. Great fear came upon everybody. And not only did fear come upon the church: 'no-one else dared join them' (Acts 5:13). There was such respect for them.

So on the way to Bethel the terror of God fell upon the towns. Wouldn't it be wonderful if the church was right with God, and a fear of God emerged in the land? What is wrong today, on both sides of the Atlantic, is that there is no fear of God. When the church gets right, the terror of God will return.

The Visitation (35:9–15)

Jacob has now arrived at his favourite spot, Bethel. The first time he just found himself there and he gave the place a new name. This time he went there under orders. Why would God ask Jacob to go back to Bethel? The answer is, for the same reason he asks each of us to see God do it again. Jacob needed a fresh visitation. And some of you need exactly this. You knew that God could do it once. Would He do it twice? I can tell you, we too will have to cleanse ourselves on the way. Our task is to be sure that God's Spirit dwells in us unhindered.

'God appeared to him again and blessed him' (verse 9). Don't tell me God won't bless us a second time! A. W. Tozer said you can have as much of God as you want.

As we close—what was the purpose of this divine visitation?

First, *to confirm Jacob's new name*. 'You will no longer be called Jacob; your name will be Israel.' Jacob meant 'heel' or 'deceiver'. Israel meant 'struggles with God'. This time God was confirming what the angel had done. And it made Jacob see that nothing had changed because of all that domestic trouble and all the difficulty that he went through and he was given to confusion and lost his temper with his sons.

There's a second reason for this visitation. It was *to renew the patriarchal oath-promise*. God said to him 'I am God Almighty. Be fruitful and increase in number. A nation and a community of nations will come from you and kings will come from your body.' And Jacob must never lose sight of God's wider purpose. He had been bedevilled by family quarrels—and a new generation emerged under his nose. It's so easy to be diverted from the things that matter. They are often unavoidable, legitimate things. But God's greater purpose was at stake, and Jacob needed to be brought back to basics. The visitation at Bethel made a statement.

And third, *to leave him, so that Jacob should continue by faith*. Look at verse 13. There was going to come a time that God would desert Jacob. We might wish that a divine visitation would go on and on and on. On the Mount of Transfiguration Peter said, 'It's good to be here.' Quite! But all supernatural manifestations end. All revivals end. We must all come down from the mountain. The Christian life is mainly lived in the valley.

God left Hezekiah 'to test him to see what was in his heart' (2 Chron. 32:31). And what was in Jacob's heart? Sheer gratitude. God had done it again. It would be a long time before something like the Bethel visitation would come again. In the meantime, he could never forget how real God had been. Such dreams, visions, visitations, prepared him for the long valley ahead.

3. Era of Dilemma
(Genesis 37:1–42:28)

I think there are two reasons that God gives unusual spiritual experiences. One is because of a special calling or plan that He has for us. The other is to prepare us for an era of dilemma. Isaiah said 'Truly you are a God who hides himself, O God and Saviour of Israel' (Isa. 45:15).

Back in the 1950s I had what I can only call a Damascus Road experience, and I came home with unusual theological views. They were foreign to my family, but I was so excited – I knew that one day God would use me. But my family didn't react in the same way.

Just a year or two before, when I accepted a pastorate at a church in Tennessee while I was a student, my grandmother gave me a brand-new 1955 Chevrolet. I was the first preacher in the family and she was proud of me. But a year or so later, when I announced to my family how I felt God was going to use me in a different theological and ecclesiastical direction, my grandmother took the car back. And I will never forget one August afternoon in 1956 when in great discouragement I said 'Lord, why? All I'm doing is following You–and look at the way it has gone down with those who are closest to me.'

I felt an urge to turn to Hebrews 12:6. I don't get urges like that every day, but I turned to it and read this: 'For whom the Lord loves He chastens and scourges every son whom He receives.'

I think that the severest form of chastening is the hiding of God's face. John Newton wrote about it:

> How tedious and tasteless the hours
> When Jesus no longer I see,
> Sweet prospects, sweet birds and sweet flowers,
> Have all lost their sweetness to me.

There comes a time when every saint experiences the hiding of God's face. I think even John the Baptist went through it, because he sent word to Jesus 'Are You really the One that should come, or do we look for another?'

It shows the paradox of the oath-level experience with God. There's a sense in which you can never doubt again and yet sometimes we do. John the Baptist couldn't have wanted greater assurance, because God had said to him 'When you see the Dove come down and remain on One, that is the One that you're going to be preaching about.' And yet he wondered if he'd got it wrong. Even Elijah, after Mount Carmel, said 'It is better for me to die than to live.' And what comfort there is when we read that Elijah was a man just like us! So we discover was Jacob, a man who had these unusual experiences: Bethel, Bethel again, Peniel – God had been so real to him. But as I said last time, it was said of Hezekiah 'The Lord left him, to test him, to see what was in his heart.'

I find it so encouraging to know that God uses ordinary men.

The Unworthy Parent (37:3–4)

Here was Jacob, doing something he ought not to have done. The day would come he would regret it so much; showing favouritism in his own family. I wonder if some of you today suffer your greatest guilt over your role as a parent? That you feel now you loved them too much or too little, that you punished too much or too little? How many of us wish we could turn the clock back and start all over again!

How many of you as you grew up said 'I'm not going to make the mistakes that my parents made with me' – but you did, and you were as bad, if not worse, than them. Jacob should have known better. He if anyone knew the scar that is left on the heart of one who's been either the favourite or the rejected child. Look at the agony he suffered by being the object of discrimination. His father preferred Esau. His mother preferred him. And it caused considerable damage. His consternation over Esau pained him for years. If anybody should have known better, it was Jacob. 'The child is father of the man,' as Wordsworth put it.

'Israel loved Joseph more than any of his other sons because he had been born to him in his old age.' He was also the son of his beloved Rachel. There's always an explanation for our behaviour, for our feelings. And so he made the 'coat of many colours' for him. There was an explanation for why he felt as he did–but try to tell that to the other sons! All behaviour is caused, but that doesn't make it right. For whatever reason, we are imperfect parents; but that doesn't change the effect it has on our children or resolve the guilt we inevitably feel.

What was the result of Joseph's coat of many colours? Unspeakable jealousy. His brothers 'hated him and could not speak a kind word to him', and rejected him. The only thing worse than giving a 'coat of many colours' was wearing it. But Joseph wore it, proud teenager aged seventeen.

That's not all. He told his dreams to his brothers. And what dreams he had! It didn't take Sigmund Freud to interpret them. The result was they hated him all the more, because of his dreams and what he said; firstly, because he was his father's favourite, secondly, because he was so insensitive when he revealed to them how God had shown him this or that.

Joseph had a marvellous gift. When it came to dreams you couldn't teach him a thing. There wasn't anything wrong with Joseph's gift, but there was a lot wrong with Joseph. He wasn't ready. It can sometimes be the same with us.

Joseph was a sovereign vessel. God said 'We need to remove him from this household,' for He had a training programme for Joseph that Jacob had not envisaged.

There was one thing that gave Jacob food for thought. 'His brothers were jealous of him but his father kept the matter in mind' (verse 11)–a reference to the dreams. It may have helped him at times across the years, for Jacob thought there was something to it.

The Unspeakable Pain (37:31–32)

Jacob thought Joseph had been killed by wild animals when in fact the brothers, instead of killing him, sold him to the Ishmaelites, never expecting to see him again. They thought of a way of covering up their sin and in so doing they presented Jacob with the greatest shock of his life. They laid before him that blood-stained coat of many colours, and they played this game: 'Dad, could this possibly be your son's robe? We found this.' It was a cruel and mean trick, but they found it easier than telling the truth.

They were their father's sons. Jacob had been the master of deceit, their sons outdid him. Isn't it a pity that our children sometimes pick up our bad habits more easily than our good ones? The pain inflicted upon Jacob was too great to describe.

The Unfounded Presumption (37:33–35)

'It is my son's robe,' said Jacob, and concluded: 'Joseph has surely been torn to pieces.' But Jacob was wrong, completely wrong. You couldn't have told him that. Do you know that his presumption led to twenty-two years of sheer agony? The evidence was indisputable, and yet the evidence was completely false.

Have you been guilty of an unfounded presumption, when you believed what you heard, or what appeared to be true—you didn't have evidence, but you thought you did? With the result that you lived for a long time, perhaps months or years, believing something that wasn't true. Perhaps you were so sure that a particular prayer couldn't be answered that you quit praying. Perhaps you were certain somebody couldn't be trusted, but you were going by hearsay and you were convinced. I think of how this has happened to me, when I was forced to admit 'I just assumed the evidence proved this. But it didn't: I thought it did.' Sometimes, indeed, you live with the wrong assumption long after the situation that caused it has been resolved.

Jesus said 'You shall know the truth and the truth will set you free' (John 8:32). Lies give way to bondage and fear–and Jacob lived twenty-two years believing a lie. I'll tell you the saddest thing of all; I was amazed when I discovered it. Do you know that never once did God speak to him, that we know of, in those twenty-two years? No Bethel, no Peniel; it was a bleak era.

It's so easy to believe what we've heard and accept information uncritically. I think of many a young theological student full of vigour, vitality, strength, enthusiasm and vision, who's done the same thing. A long time ago they looked at the evidence presented by some liberal scholar and decided that the Bible was a faulty document that couldn't be believed any more. They graduated and spent years without effectiveness, even if they went into the ministry–all because of false evidence. I've seen it happen again and again.

Jacob said 'It's my son's robe. Joseph has surely been torn to pieces.' He was so sure he was right–but he was wrong. Perhaps you need to look again: who is it you don't trust at present because of what somebody told you? Are you so sure you've been right? And what about the unanswered prayer? In Luke 1 Zechariah, who was to be father of John the Baptist, was suddenly visited by Gabriel, the archangel. Gabriel said 'Zechariah, don't be afraid, your prayer is heard.'

'Prayer?... What, what do you mean? What prayer?'

'You were praying for a son.'

'Oh!' says Zechariah. 'But that was twenty, twenty-five years ago. Have you taken a look at my wife lately? Obviously she's not going to be bearing children.'

Because God hadn't answered the prayer, Zechariah concluded it wasn't going to happen. He had the evidence, but he was wrong. Zechariah says 'Your prayer is heard' (can I just say, it's a reminder that any prayer prayed in the will of God will be answered.) And what should have been Zechariah's finest hour, with a promised baby on the way, left him blushing and dumb. All because he had believed it wasn't going to happen.

We are to re-examine the evidence. Consider how much you have believed. It was an unfounded presumption. Jacob should have remembered Bethel. I find that when God leaves me, to test me, it is always so embarrassing: there's so little left! Jeremiah was right, 'The heart is deceitful above all things, and desperately wicked: who can know it?' (Jer. 17:9 AV). Paul said 'In my flesh dwelleth no good thing' (Rom. 7:18). But what God was doing was hemming in Jacob in such a way that he would never be able to take any credit for what God did.

The Unavoidable Plight (41:56—42:2)

Egypt's prosperity was objective fact, but subjectively nobody in Canaan would have thought Joseph was alive, much less that he was Prime Minister of Egypt.

But Joseph was sold to the Ishmaelites, who sold him to the Egyptians, who made Joseph part of the household of Potiphar, an officer in the Egyptian army. He endeared himself to his master, progressed, and was brought right into the house to live. Joseph, a sovereign vessel, without Jacob's manipulation, was being trained for greatness.

He had to pass two tests before God could trust him with the responsible position. First, *overcoming sexual temptation*. Potiphar's wife attempted to seduce him, and he refused. 'How could I do this thing and sin against God?' What amazes me about Joseph is that he resisted Potiphar's wife in a country where, even if he gave in and was caught, at least the people who mattered to him, his father and brothers, wouldn't know about it. Many of you have resisted sexual temptation only because you didn't want to get caught, or because you were afraid who would hear of it if you were discovered. But Joseph had the opportunity for the perfect affair. Why did he reject Potiphar's wife? He said 'God knows about it. How can I do this and sin against God?' And next thing we know, Joseph is in the dungeon.

Test number two for Joseph—sovereign vessel—and that is *refusing to be a manipulator*. Pharaoh's butler and baker join him in the dungeon. One day he notices they both look very sad, and they explain: 'We had bad dreams last night.' Joseph's ears perk up. He thinks 'At long last my gift is going to be discovered!'

So he says to the butler 'Your dream means that you're

going to be restored to your position.' To the baker he says 'Sorry about you,' but to the butler, 'Now look, you're going to be restored to your position in three days...remember me. Joseph. J-o-s-e-p-h. I've done nothing wrong, I don't deserve to be here. Remember me to Pharaoh.' And God looked down from heaven and said 'Oh, Joseph, I wish you hadn't said that...you're going to need a couple of more years.'

The Bible says that love doesn't boast, because there's no fear in love. Perfect love casts out fear; and when you're living in love, you're not going to try to pull strings or nudge the arm of Providence. You let God do it. And God says to Joseph 'You're not ready.'

The time came when Joseph forgave his brothers, forgave God, for letting it all happen. There was a knock on the door and he found himself shaving and preparing to face the Pharaoh, who had had his own dream. The butler remembered. Joseph interpreted the dream and the Pharaoh was so impressed that he put him in charge of all Egypt. Overnight Joseph was made Prime Minister of Egypt. A sovereign vessel! God did it without Jacob. Joseph prophesied to Pharaoh about the seven years of plenty and the seven years of famine, and advised him to stockpile food during the years of plenty so that in the years of famine he would have food to feed the world. That impressed the Pharaoh.

Now Joseph's prophecy was coming to pass. The seven years of famine were setting in. Only Egypt was prepared for it. The whole world was affected by it, and the famine therefore reached Canaan.

And we see in 42:1 the unavoidable plight. Jacob needed Egypt. Who could have known that the hand of God was behind it all? Who would have thought the day would come that Jacob would be so hemmed in that he would have no choice but to recognise that Egypt was in some way the way of the future? Do you know what it is to be hemmed in? 'He has walled me in so that I cannot escape; he has weighed me down with chains' (Lam. 3:7).

Perhaps you are like that. You've been hemmed in, you've been boxed into a corner, there's no way out. Perhaps you feel like the Children of Israel; wedged in a pocket at the Red

Sea, Pharaoh's army coming from one direction, the Red Sea behind—they didn't know what to do. But the unavoidable plight is God's signal to us. When there's nothing we can do but trust Him, God takes things out of our hands so that we are forced to do what we said we'd never do. Appealing to Egypt was unthinkable for Jacob, but he had no choice. Egypt was the way of the future.

The Unhappy Predicament (42:29–37)

Now matters were going from bad to worse. It was one thing to have lost Joseph, but now Jacob was having to forfeit Benjamin. Benjamin, also Rachel's son, had replaced Joseph in his father's affections—Jacob was making the same mistake again. And he was also being hemmed in again. He was told 'Release Benjamin or we're all going to die.' It was an unhappy predicament.

Meanwhile, the brothers had faced the Prime Minister of Egypt. Of course, they didn't know it was Joseph. Many years had passed. The Prime Minister spoke officiously to them in Egyptian, through an interpreter. He accused them of being spies. They went home with food; but next time, they must bring Benjamin. And Simeon had been held as a ransom. The whole family was now hemmed in.

Jacob lost his temper. 'You have deprived me of my children. Joseph is no more. Simeon is no more. Now you want to take Benjamin. Everything is against me.' He blamed them for everything. And of course in a sense he was right, much more than he knew. We may be right in what we say when we lose our tempers, but that puts us in the wrong. When we grieve the Spirit we always feel justified at the time. And when we lose our tempers we feel justified at the time. It always seems right at the time ... blaming his sons for everything, Jacob's anger turned to self-pity, 'Everything is against me.'

The devil loves to get us wallowing in self-pity; and it is a fault from which it is very difficult to be extricated. I would prefer to deal with almost any other pastoral problem. When a person is full of self-pity they can be almost unreachable. But Paul tells us 'When you see a brother overtaken in a fault you who are spiritual restore such a one in the spirit of

meekness, considering yourself lest you also be tempted'
(Gal. 6:1). And self-pity is a fault that we sometimes have to
deal with.

Reuben, the first-born, made an effort to salvage the
situation (verse 37). 'You may put both of my sons to death,
if I do not bring him back to you. Entrust him to my care, and
I will bring him back.' Reuben was once willing to leave
Joseph in a pit to die, so he is in no position to be self-
righteous. We're told 'considering yourself lest you also be
tempted'. That means, when you're helping another person,
don't be self-righteous because you could be in the same
situation. Reuben was in no position to be self-righteous.
And we all have skeletons in our cupboards. There's not a
single one of us who's earned the right to be self-righteous.

Reuben offered both his sons as guarantee. Jacob said 'No
deal.' Reuben's efforts met with temporary failure.

The Unguarded Pledge (42:38)

'My son will not go down there with you . . . He is the only one
left.' That's one of the harshest statements a father could
ever make to a family. How do you suppose it made the other
ten brothers feel?

The truth is that Jacob was ridden with guilt. Often when
we strike out at somebody it's because we ourselves feel
guilty. The old patriarch, 130 years old, made a rash vow:
'Benjamin will not go down with you.' We've all been guilty
of the unguarded pledge. Never say 'Never'; you may have to
eat your words. But Jacob could not bear any other option.

And yet, when you read between the lines, he was beginning to soften. 'If harm comes to him on the journey you are
taking, you will bring my grey head down to the grave in
sorrow.' It shows that he was beginning to give in just a little
bit, and admit the possibility of it all. But the older we get the
more set we are in our ways, and Jacob was an old man
indeed.

One of the things I pray for myself is that God will enable
me, by the Holy Spirit, to be open–an uncommon quality, as
one gets older. I wonder, have you made an unguarded
pledge, a rash vow? Have you gone on record as saying
something and dare not change your mind now because

people will find out? You had good reason for taking your stand; now you're digging in your heels. We're all so proud! Yet God has a way of changing the oldest and hardest of us. But it is painful, because we're so full of pride.

Jacob tried to save face–'Go back and buy us a little more food' (43:2), as if to forget what he'd just been told. He tried to deny the obvious; he knew what he had to do. He pretended he hadn't heard them. May I ask, is God telling someone here today 'You need to change'? Are those closest to you praying that you will? Are you playing games with yourself? You do see the truth in your heart of hearts, but you just can't admit that you might have been wrong. Are we so entrenched that we are unteachable? Are we really motivated by pride rather than principle?

Now Judah gets into the act (43:3) But Jacob wasn't giving in easily: 'Why did you bring this trouble on me by telling the man you had another brother?' He still wanted to blame them. Is your unwillingness to change rooted in the need to blame someone else? But (verse 7) they were guilty simply of telling the truth.

The Underwritten Promise (43:8–14)

Judah continues to speak to his father in what is, to my mind, one of the most moving sections in the whole story. For one thing, nobody could have known at the time that out of the loins of Judah would come the promised Messiah, the Son of God. Judah is perhaps unconsciously speaking prophetically in verse 8. In the Authorised Version we have a quaint, if not archaic, word–but it's a tremendous one that appears in many of our hymns–where Judah says 'I will be a "surety" for him'. That is what the blood of Jesus was, shed on the cross of Calvary. Sprinkled on the mercy seat, it became precisely that: the surety, the guarantee. Hebrews 7:22 tells us that He was made the guarantee, the surety of a better covenant.

And He came from the line of Judah. John, on the Isle of Patmos, heard a voice saying: 'Do not weep! See, the Lion of the tribe of Judah, the Root of David, has triumphed' (Rev. 5:5).

What was happening here? Judah was now saying 'You

can hold me personally responsible for him.' That is what
Jesus said to the Father while He was hanging on the cross:
'Blame Me. I will take the sins of the world. Blame Me.'
Isaiah 53:6 says 'The Lord has laid on him the iniquity of us
all.' On one occasion Calvin exclaimed 'If anyone asks how I
know I am elect, I answer, "Christ is better than a thousand
testimonies to me!" ' Charles Spurgeon said, 'If I go to hell,
I'll go to hell trusting the blood of Jesus.' And so Judah could
say 'Blame me. Hold me personally responsible.'

Our salvation is based upon this. For this is what we must
do: put all of our eggs into one basket. Jesus said to the
Father, 'Blame me.' God took Him at His word. God
punished Jesus instead of me. He took the full responsibility
for the sins of the world.

Judah's plea convinced an argumentative Jacob. 'Take
your brother and go back...As for me' (a little remnant of
self-pity here) 'if I am bereaved, I am bereaved' (verse 13).

The Unbelievable Providence (45:25–26)

'They told him "Joseph is still alive! In fact, he is ruler of all
Egypt." ' Jacob was stunned. He did not believe them. Do
you remember the worst day of your life? I think we can
safely say when Jacob's was. It was that day of unfounded
presumption when he looked at the bloodstained coat of
many colours and said, 'It's Joseph's. A wild beast has
devoured him.'

That was the end of Jacob's world, or so he thought. There
was not much that Jacob could be happy about now. All that
he had to live for, it seemed, was gone. Nobody could put a
smile on his face. Yes, he remembered Joseph's dreams. Yes,
he remembered Bethel. But that was so long ago. It had been
so long since he had seen God work. He wasn't prepared for
the news that was coming. If anything, he was prepared for
the worst. Benjamin wouldn't return. And the best thing that
could happen, in his mind, was that Benjamin would come
back and they'd have food again.

This was the most mind-boggling day in Salvation history
since the time of Abraham.

In the meantime, the sons were shaken with the news.
They found themselves in the presence of the Prime Minister,

when suddenly he said, 'Make everyone leave my presence' (45:1). They were alone with him when he made himself known to them. He even made the interpreter leave. Suddenly, he began to speak Hebrew to them, and tears rolled down his cheeks as he said 'I'm Joseph. I'm Joseph. Is my father still alive?' And he began to weep so loudly that the Egyptians heard him, and Pharaoh's household heard about it.

His brothers were unable to answer him because they were terrified at his presence. But what Joseph did in that moment was to show them something he'd learned in the dungeon. He'd forgiven God, for all that God let happen. He'd forgiven God for letting Potiphar's wife do what she did. He'd forgiven his brothers. He was a man who was free.

Many years ago I went through what was the greatest trial of my life. I told an old friend, 'You won't believe what these people have done to me.' He counselled me: 'RT, you must totally forgive them. For until you do, you will be in chains. Release them, and you will be released.' Faithful are the wounds of a friend! Nobody had talked to me like that in my life. It was the most emancipating experience I ever had.

That is what Joseph had to do—totally forgive. How do we know he totally forgave them? Well, the first thing he did was to make everybody leave the room. Why? Well, he's going to get them to move to Egypt, and he doesn't want anybody in Egypt to know what they did to him. The proof you've totally forgiven the one who has hurt you is that you don't let anybody know what they did to you. As long as you want somebody to know what they did to you, you haven't totally forgiven. Joseph was protecting them.

Another proof that we've totally forgiven is that we don't want those who have hurt us to be afraid of us. Joseph says 'Come close to me, I'm your brother, don't be distressed.' He didn't want them to be afraid. When we haven't forgiven somebody we want to keep them intimidated, a little bit afraid of us. But Joseph says 'Come close.'

Another proof is that we not only want them to know we have forgiven them, we want them to be able to forgive themselves. So verse 5: 'Do not be distressed and do not be angry with yourselves.' We sometimes say to people 'Well, I forgive you for what you did, but I hope you feel bad about it.' That just shows how far we've forgiven them.

And then perhaps the ultimate proof that we've totally forgiven, is that we let those who have hurt us save face. Joseph said to them 'Do not be angry with yourselves for selling me here, because it was to save lives that God sent me ahead of you.' It's Joseph's way of saying 'If I'd have been in your shoes I'd have done the same thing. Somebody had to go first. I was just the one selected. You may have meant it for evil but God meant it for good. Don't be angry. God's behind the whole thing.'

His brothers can't believe that they have been forgiven. The way we show we've forgiven another is to see the hand of God in it all. 'You know very well that if you were in the same situation you'd have done the same thing.' If you don't think that, then you're self-righteous and you haven't really seen the picture of your own heart. But Joseph was a transformed man. This was something God was doing, without the help of Jacob.

So these ten sons were shaken with the news. That officious Prime Minister was none other than Joseph. He had totally forgiven them. They all wept together. They were given instructions: 'You tell my father to come and live in security in Egypt, and don't quarrel on the way.'

On their journey back to Canaan they had much to absorb, it seemed too much to take in. The big question was, would the old patriarch believe it all? Perhaps they had a discussion how best to convince him. It was a day of days, a day of staggering bliss, the happiest day of their father's life— once he believed it.

We're not told which one broke the news. Nobody could be surprised at the old man's reaction. He was stunned—some think he collapsed. The old patriarch had two things to absorb. One, that Joseph was alive. That alone was incredible. And that he happens to be Prime Minister in Egypt. Jacob couldn't take it in. It was just the way the disciples felt when they heard that Jesus was raised from the dead.

And yet that is the essence of the gospel. To think that our Lord died on a cross and that we are saved by what He did, plus nothing! Sheer trust in what He did on the cross assures us of heaven.

Jacob's reaction was 'It can't be so.'

The Undoubted Proof (45:27–28)

They told him everything. It seemed like idle tales. Jacob listened in disbelief, hoping it was true, but what convinced him? 'When he saw the carts Joseph had sent to carry him back, the spirit of their father Jacob revived.' It must be so. They had come down from none other than Joseph himself. And the traumatised spirit of Jacob revived.

Now he had undoubted proof. No unfounded presumption now, the twenty-two years of dilemma were over. They say life begins at forty, but for Jacob life was to begin at 130. The manipulative, stubborn, grandson of Abraham had something to live for–it was better than ever.

I sometimes think that God loves to save the best surprises for old age. Do you think that the best days are past? Ecclesiastes 7:10 contradicts you. For Jacob, for you, the best is yet to come. The argumentative, inflexible, entrenched old man said 'I am convinced. Joseph is alive. I will go and see him before I die.'

Great is Thy faithfulness, O God my Father;
There is no shadow of turning with Thee.
Thou changest not; Thy compassions, they fail not.
As Thou hast been, Thou forever will be.

All's well that ends well! No dilemma now.

4. Era of Destiny
(Genesis 46:1–49:33)

I've been almost overwhelmed by your kindness to us here at Keswick, and by your acceptance; I can't tell you how much I've enjoyed it. Louise and I have been thrilled to be here, and we will never forget it.

Today we come to our final study: 'Era of Destiny'. The task of every generation is to discover the direction in which the Sovereign Redeemer is moving, and to move in that direction too.

Ecclesiastes 7:10: 'Do not say, "Why were the old days better than these?".' If only we would learn: these are the good old days–no matter how old we are! And who would have thought that Jacob, aged 130, was now at the beginning of a new era, that his most exciting days lay ahead? At long last everything comes together for him. He rediscovers what he should have remembered: that God is still on the throne. His long patriarchal nightmare is over. No dilemma now! And he begins to pick up the thread that holds all together.

God said 'I will never leave you, nor forsake you' (Deut. 31:6, Heb. 13.5). Jesus said 'I am with you always, to the very end of the age' (Matt. 28:20). Jacob said 'I am convinced my son Joseph, is still alive. I will go and see him before I die.' It meant that God had His hand on his son Joseph all along. It meant that God had a purpose in his losing Joseph. It meant that the ancient promise to Abraham still stood. The renewal of the promise to Isaac still stood and so did everything that had been promised to Jacob.

It was really true what Isaac said: 'Jacob shall be blessed', what God said to Rebekah: 'The elder shall serve the younger.' Never mind that Jacob stole his brother's birthright and Isaac had been deceived. God had been sovereignly at the bottom of it all. It seemed too good to be true, but it was true. 'I am convinced, my son Joseph is still alive. I will go and see him before I die.' So Jacob made immediate plans to move house.

Anticipating Change (46:1)

Jacob now experienced another trauma. It's said you can't teach an old dog new tricks, and we're talking about a very old man. And any psychologist will tell you that moving house is a severe process of change at any age.

All of us are congenitally opposed to change, and the older we are the more difficult it becomes. Young people, remember; you will be old one day. You may be impatient now with those who resist change, but you're going to be like that one day!

Well, Jacob–aged 130–was having to accept the new and different. The problem was compounded; he had to leave Canaan, the Promised Land. It was a wrench for him not only emotionally but theologically. How could he leave the land? And of all places, to go to Egypt, where Abraham his grandfather got into trouble! To move to Egypt seemed like a betrayal. And what would Isaac think, to whom God had said, 'Do not go down to Egypt; live in the land where I tell you to live. Stay in this land' (26:2). And now Jacob is being told he's got to go to Egypt. 'How can I do this, to my ancestors?'

Do you know, the reason many of us are opposed to change is that we feel we're betraying those who went before us. And so one of the questions we encounter this morning is: 'How does God enable us to accept the new and different?'

Assured Confirmation (46:2–4)

One of the ways God prepares us for the new and different is
by providing an attractive alternative to the bleak and dismal
past. Keep in mind first that Jacob was preoccupied with
sorrow and self-pity for the past twenty-two years. Second,
that for twenty-two years he was operating totally in a sphere
of the false, making an assumption based upon inconclusive
evidence: Joseph was in fact not dead at all. And third, that
so far as we know he had no experience with God during
those twenty-two years. All of his great experiences pre-date
Joseph's departure.

The truth is, God hadn't been real to Jacob for a long
time. One of the reasons that Jacob became open to the new
and different is that the present and immediate past wasn't
really all that great. Some of us are opposed to change; but if
we're to be honest, what we're holding on to isn't all that
great either. May I ask you to be honest? How long has it
been since God was real to you? And is God giving you a hint
that the present and the immediate past isn't all that great?

Well, God prepared Jacob for the new and different by a
restoration of the old experiences with God he once had.
'And God spoke to Israel in a vision at night and said "Jacob!
Jacob!" ' What a sound that was! It was beginning to happen
again, and that was proof enough to Jacob.

But it didn't happen until he started out; then God spoke
to him. The trouble with many of us is we want God to do it
and then we will obey. God is asking us to do what He tells us
to do, and when He hems us in and gives us every hint that
He's wanting us to move on, we're not going to see something happen until we make a move.

So it happened again. God spoke to him, in 'a vision at
night'–meaning, a dream. You recall on the day of Pentecost
how Peter quoted from Joel: 'In the last days, God says, I will
pour out my Spirit on all people. Your sons and daughters
will prophesy, your young men will see visions, your old men
will dream dreams' (Acts 2:17). I used to wonder why it says
'old men will dream dreams'. But we saw the Era of Dreams
a few days ago, when Jacob was younger. When we're young
we dream, we look ahead, we fantasise about how it's going
to be; often when people get older they don't dream any

more. But God says 'I'm going to give you a new beginning–
old men will dream dreams.'

Now Jacob, having thought that the past was behind him
and there was nothing to look forward to, began to dream
again. And that was proof enough to Jacob. No more
pseudo-guilt regarding his ancestors: in fact God said 'Don't
be afraid to go down to Egypt, for I will make you into a
great nation there.' The Era of Destiny was inaugurated by a
new dream. Something to look forward to. And yet the truth
is, that new and different situation was forced upon Jacob: it
wasn't something he was seeking. He was prepared to live in
Canaan, accepting inconclusive evidence, for ever.

I said the other day that I am by nature a coward, and a
traditionalist. I have accepted the new and different now and
then, but only for one reason; God put a pistol to my head.
Jacob, too, had no choice. There was no food in Canaan,
only in Egypt. All his prejudice against Egypt had to be
discarded, and yet there came this happy bonus–he would
see Joseph again.

How do you know the new and different comes from God?
I, for one, don't want change for its own sake. How do you
know the new, and different, really is from God?

Four things.

First, God is real again.

Second, there is continuity with the past. No change that
comes from God will result in discontinuity with the God of
the Bible and the faith of our fathers. 'I am God, the God of
your father.' It was the same God.

Third, there is a sweet clarification of the past, present and
future. One of the things that amazes me–it was there in our
first Bible reading–is that God's intervention clarified something for Jacob that he must have wondered about for a long
time. Do you remember, God said 'I am with you and will
watch over you wherever you go, and I will bring you back to
this land' (28:15)? That was an odd thing to say. Why would
God say 'I will bring you back to this land'? It could only
mean that God knew then that one day he'd be leaving so the
promise was he would be brought back.

Carried back, after he died–but he would be brought
back. Perhaps some of us have a promise given to us and we

wonder why God hasn't fulfilled it. But He will keep His word. And He has a way of clarifying what is in our past and the scripture we didn't understand. Jesus said, 'If anyone chooses to do God's will, he will find out whether my teaching comes from God' (John 7:17). Jacob could see now there was reason for that verse way back.

You know, I expect that revival is coming, I believe it with all my heart. But it doesn't mean that I'll be here when it happens. God may give me the vision, and someone else see it. Jacob came back, but they carried him back. Yet it happened! The proof that you are in God's will is that eventually the things of the past will be clarified. And the promise regarding the future was: 'There I will make you into a great nation.'

And fourth, Jacob saw God working, without his own intervention. Jacob was the world's greatest manipulator. It was one of the reasons for his guilt. There was always a natural explanation for so much that happened to him. He used people as objects for his own goals. He needed to see God work, apart from him.

Why do you suppose he gave Joseph the coat of many colours? Because Jacob the manipulator wanted to give him a head start. But the plan backfired, and Joseph becoming Prime Minister of Egypt was something that happened outside Jacob's control. I take great comfort from this, that God can do for our own children what we utterly fail to do. What enabled Jacob to accept change was that he'd seen God do something, in such a way that he knew it was totally out of his hands.

By the way, he made a clean break: 'So Israel set out with all that was his.' He went from the past to the future and accepted the new and different.

Affectionate Celebration (46:29–30)

Jacob's family now totalled seventy. It would seem that Jacob got to Goshen before Joseph, Judah having led the way. Goshen may not have looked much at first: it may have been the fat of the land to the Egyptians, but to Jacob it was a strange place. Where was Joseph? Well, Joseph was simply waiting for the signal from his officials that the family had arrived. But Jacob got there first.

Sometimes when God does something new and different, you want some kind of spectacular beginning. But it's often so uneventful that you think 'Is this it?'. God told Abraham to go to a country and he would be guided; then Abraham arrived and there was no great welcoming ceremony. No voice from heaven said 'This is it!'

When I was called as Minister of Westminster Chapel the Secretary telephoned me to tell me what the result of the vote was: 'Well, we've called you to be our pastor.'

I said 'Well, that's good.'

He said 'Are you going to accept?'

I said 'Yes, I think I am!'

He said 'Good.'

I said 'Well, when do I become the minister?'

He said 'You're the minister now.'

I said 'That's it? What about the induction service?'

'Well, do you need that?'

I thought 'Dr Lloyd Jones says "They didn't do it for me, I don't know why they should do it for you!" '. And I thought, 'Well – this is it!'

Often, you know, beginnings can be so unspectacular . . .

Nobody's there. Then Jacob arrives, stoop-shouldered, perhaps with failing eyesight, leaning on his staff, looking in all directions. His eleven sons begin erecting tents in Goshen. Jacob peers into the distance. An elaborate chariot, trailing dust, comes into view. It halts among the tents. Old Jacob hobbles forward. The Prime Minister, now forty years old, gets out of his chariot and look around. He sees an old man making his way towards him and walks briskly to him. He begins to run, they recognise each other, stretching out their arms . . . and Joseph 'threw his arms around his father and wept for a long time.' Joseph had already shown himself a man who was unafraid to cry; on this occasion he let himself go.

Israel said to Joseph, 'Now I am ready to die, since I have seen for myself that you are still alive.' Until then Jacob was afraid to die. There were too many loose ends in his life. But in this Era of Destiny everything came together. Until now it was surely too good to be true, but not now.

Are you ready to die? We're not ready to live until we're ready to die. Jacob was ready to die: he was also ready to live, and he did–for seventeen more years.

Apprehensive Ceremony (47:1–10)

The time was approaching for Jacob and his sons to appear before royalty. They were going to need instructions: how to act, what to say. They were going into the presence of the Pharaoh.

Joseph briefed them (46:33), and it happened as he had said. Everything went according to plan. Pharaoh said to Joseph, 'Your father and your brothers have come to you, and the land of Egypt is before you; settle your father and your brothers in the best part of the land. Let them live in Goshen.'

Two things stand out in this ceremony. First, Jacob's sense of inferiority to his own ancestors. 'My years have been few and difficult, and they do not equal the years of the pilgrimage of my fathers.' Perhaps none of us feels equal to those whom God has blessed and used in the past. Joseph was aware that his father knew all of these things and he was making it as easy as he could for him, because he knew that Jacob was ever conscious that he had done nothing to deserve such blessing and honour.

The second thing that stands out is that Jacob blessed Pharaoh. He wasn't used to foreign visitors blessing him: they always came to him for some kind of help. Pharaoh had never known anything like that before. He couldn't have known that it was the best thing that could happen to him: that the patriarchal blessing had tremendous power.

Apparent Contradiction (48:17–20)

Jacob's life was now drawing to a close. Joseph fervently wanted his father to bless his sons.

Manassah, the first-born, and Ephraim, the second, were sons of Joseph's Egyptian wife. The good news was that Jacob accepted them as his own; the disquieting news was that Jacob put Ephraim before Manassah. He did it by switching his hands. Joseph had manoeuvred Manassah so that Jacob's right hand would fall on the first-born and his left on Ephraim. From earliest times the right hand was symbolic: it is still the one we shake when greeting each other. In the Bible the right hand is always symbolic of power: 'Sit thou at my right hand, until I make thine enemies thy footstool' (Psa. 110:1 AV), or John's vision at Patmos: 'When I saw him, I fell at his feet as dead. And he laid his right hand upon me, saying unto me, Fear not; I am the first and the last' (Rev. 1:17 AV).

So Joseph the anxious father was determined that his first-born should be blessed with the right hand. But suddenly the old patriarch placed his right hand on Ephraim's head and his left hand on Manassah's. When Joseph saw this he was displeased (verse 17), so he tried to move his father's hand: 'My father, I don't think you understand. This one is the first-born. Put your right hand on his head.'

But Jacob knew exactly what he was doing, and refused. 'I know, my son, I know. He too will become a people, and he too will become great. Nevertheless, his younger brother will be greater than he, and his descendants will become a group of nations.' So he put Ephraim ahead of Manassah.

History was repeating itself. Like father, like son. Jacob had an opportunity to walk in his father's steps. It had been hard for old Isaac to bless Jacob and not Esau; now Jacob himself must be impartial. We all know how much he loved Joseph, but Jacob had a chance to show he loved God more. He followed the Spirit and gave the superior blessing to Ephraim. Jacob was doing for Ephraim what God had done for him. He was passing sovereign grace to Joseph's second son. At long last Jacob was being no respecter of persons: all's well that ends well!

Often we have no idea who will be blessed by God. Man looks on the outward appearance, God looks on the heart. To know those upon whom the genuine anointing is resting takes an awful lot of discernment. Do you know about the skeleton in the cupboard of Regent's Park College, the Baptist College at Oxford? It used to be in London, hence the name; and a young man called Charles Haddon Spurgeon applied for entrance into the College and they said 'No deal. We see no gift in you.'

Perhaps spirituality might be defined as closing the time gap between our perception of somebody, and God's perception of that person? I've given three definitions of spirituality this week. 'Closing the time gap between moment and memory'; 'Closing the time gap between sin and repentance'; and now, 'Closing the gap between our perception of somebody, and God's perception of that person'. How long does it take you to recognise an anointed man?

Jacob's hand on Ephraim made a difference. Joseph had to accept it.

Absolute Conferment (49:1–28)

We're coming to the end of our study of Jacob. We now look briefly at the conferment of his blessing upon the twelve sons, to the twelve tribes of Israel. We've seen again and again: the patriarchal blessing mattered. So one by one, in order of birth, the twelve sons of Israel queue up to get an absolute conferment. We're not going to look at each one, but three things stand out in Chapter 49.

The first is *the questionable blessing that Jacob gave to his own first-born Reuben* (verses 3–4). Not much of a blessing there! But what we have here is Jacob by-passing his first-born. You see, Jacob had by-passed Joseph's first-born and given the superior blessing to Ephraim. Now he was being consistent; he did the same thing with his own first-born. But Jacob put his seal on a new way of thinking that is so new that many of us are never quite prepared for it.

God said to the prophet Isaiah, 'My ways are higher than your ways: my thoughts higher than your thoughts.' We're not prepared for how differently God thinks to what we expect. He seems always to be way ahead of us. And it takes us years to see that what God was doing really was His deliberate act.

Second, *the messianic blessing to Judah*. Of all the twelve tribes of Israel, to get a blessing like this! If you didn't know, to whom would you have thought Jacob would give the greatest blessing? Joseph, no doubt. But lo and behold, it comes to Judah, Jacob's fourth son, born of Leah the wife he never appreciated.

There's so much more in this blessing (49:8–12) than we now have time to discuss. But what we have is clear irrefutable evidence for infallible revelation, hundreds and hundreds of years in advance of the time. Royalty would come from Judah's loins, fulfilled in David's kingship. Messiah would come from the tribe of Judah–being the root of David, as we see in Revelation 5. Who would have predicted that from Judah's loins would come the Lord Jesus Christ?

And so in this moment, Jacob got it right. He by-passed his beloved Joseph, by-passed his first-born and singled out one whom nobody would have suspected to be the way of the future.

Third, *the lack of long-term blessing given to Joseph's offspring*. It was a wonderful affirmation, yes. But there was nothing to guarantee perpetuity, such as was given to Judah alone. The point is that Jacob's blessing was according to the Spirit. No manipulation now: he had come a long way. Jacob was at total peace with himself.

Awesome Contemplation (Hebrews 11:21)

We end where we began, at Hebrews 11:21. In that famous chapter Jacob gets only one verse. Surely the man whose name was changed to Israel deserved more space than that? But no: Hebrews 11.21 says it all. 'By faith Jacob, when he was dying, blessed each of Joseph's sons and worshipped as he leaned on the top of his staff.'

For twenty-two years Jacob gave up hope of blessing all of his sons. For twenty-two years he thought he had let Abraham down, that he had let his father Isaac down. It looked like things had gone badly wrong. He blamed himself. He thought he'd lost Simeon, he was afraid he was going to lose Benjamin, and the thought of blessing Joseph was out of the question. But we're told in Hebrews 11.21 that he not only blessed Joseph, he blessed Joseph's sons. All's well that ends well! How did Jacob do it? Well, he did it as he should have done it in the first place in respect of Joseph.

I am constantly amazed at God's graciousness in giving Jacob a second chance, in allowing him to save face before the end. In the beginning he should have been an impartial father. He should have stopped playing the manipulator. But God gave him a second chance before it was over.

It hurt him to disappoint Joseph, but this was part of the test; when God gives a second chance He doesn't say it will be easy. But He loves to do it. And Jacob now had a chance to show impartiality after all.

Sometimes, to show that we really do love Him, we will say 'Lord, I love You'. But twenty-four hours later we are again ashamed of something we've done. 'Did I do that? I can't believe I did . . .' And God lets us.

Simon Peter told Jesus, 'I will follow You. I will never desert You.' Jesus said 'You will.' 'Oh no, You don't know me, I love You'. Did you ever notice that misleading chapter division at the end of John 13: are you aware that when Jesus said to Peter 'Before the cock crows you will deny Me', He also said 'Let not your heart be troubled, you believe God, believe also in Me'?

You see, God knew what Peter would do. And Peter felt so ashamed. But I've always felt I understood Acts 5:41: 'The apostles left the Sanhedrin, rejoicing because they had been counted worthy of suffering disgrace for the Name.' They felt they had let him down: they all forsook him and fled. Now they were just looking for any opportunity to show they loved God. And when they were whipped and scoffed at, they left the Sanhedrin and nudged each other saying 'Can you believe this? It's happening to us. We're getting to suffer the shame of His name!' It's a wonderful thing when God lets us have a second chance.

That's what Joseph did with his brothers. It's often thought that when he put his cup in Benjamin's bag he was being a bit naughty. Don't you know why he did that? It was to let his brothers see that they had changed. They could have left Benjamin to take the blame and gone on home–but they all came back with him. They had changed.

Some of you are wanting to know, more than anything else, that you really love God. God came to Jonah a second time, and God comes to us today. It is amazing how He lets us save face and have a second chance to show we really have put Him first. All's well that ends well!

Incidentally, no-one knows for sure where the writer of the Hebrews found that he 'worshipped leaning on the top of his staff'. Genesis 49 doesn't mention it explicitly, but somehow the writer of Hebrews knew. Perhaps he saw a vision of Jacob: we know by the Spirit, he got into Jacob's skin. And I think the writer of the Epistle to the Hebrews knew that never had a man felt so unworthy, so guilty, at one stage – and never had a man felt so thankful. And I suspect there was a time when old Jacob just went on his own and stood, leaning on the top of his staff, and worshipped.

What makes us worship? When we see our gracious God as the backdrop to our folly. When our feeling of gratitude is beyond the capability of words. When all we can do is whisper 'Thank You'. Some of us become so sophisticated that we forget the pit from which we were dug. I've often identified with David as God occasionally reminded him, 'I chose you from the pasture, I chose you from being a shepherd, don't you ever forget it.' There came a time when Nathan the prophet said to David 'You're not going to be able to build the Temple, David. God said He's been pretty good to you: but you can't build the Temple.' David went in and sat before the Lord and said 'Who am I, O Lord God? What is my family that You have brought me this far?'

I found out something the other day I didn't know before. Several months ago I decided to spend time every day reading one of John Newton's hymns. He wrote one every week – there's discipline! – basing it on his text for the week's sermon. One Sunday he planned to preach from 1 Chronicles 17:16, which describes the occasion when King David went in and sat before the Lord. That week John Newton wrote 'Amazing Grace'. The third verse comes right out of this text:

> Through many dangers, toils and snares
> I have already come,
> 'Tis grace that brought me safe this far
> And grace will lead me home.

Jacob, leaning on the top of his staff, reflected: that which once gave him the greatest sense of guilt, now gave him the greatest sense of gratitude. God had sanctified to him his deepest distress. All that was wrong in his relationship with Joseph became the very springboard of the good he had seen.

One last thing. Jacob never appreciated Leah–but are you aware of his last words? He gave these instructions: 'I am about to be gathered to my people. Bury me with my fathers in the cave in the field of Ephron the Hittite' (49:29). He adds 'There Abraham and his wife Sarah were buried. There Isaac and his wife Rebekah were buried, and there I buried Leah' (49:31). He put that right as well.

> Depth of Mercy–can there be
> Mercy still reserved for me?
> Can my God His wrath forbear?
> Me, the chief of sinners, spare?
>
> There for me the Saviour stands,
> Shows His wounds and spreads His hands,
> God is Love, I know, I feel,
> Jesus lives and loves me still.
> All's well that ends well!

(Charles Wesley)

Parables of the Kingdom

by Dr Roy Clements

1. The Seed of Change
(Luke 8:1–15)

They were coming from all directions, like fans converging on
a football ground. They came alone, they came in groups.
Husbands brought their wives, mothers brought their children, youths brought their mates. Some seemed to have
brought their whole town with them. They came because
they were sick and handicapped and thought He might heal
them. They came because they were poor and oppressed and
thought He might deliver them. They came because they
were bored and curious and thought He might amuse them.
They came – well, some of them would have had a hard job
explaining why exactly they had come, except that everybody
else was coming.

But with whatever company and with whatever motivation
they came, there was one word on Jesus' lips which intrigued
and excited them all: 'kingdom'.

'The kingdom of God has come.' That's what they said He
was preaching. For the rural masses of Galilee those words
were like sparks on dry tinder.

Every society has its dream of a better world: the classless
society, the American dream, Utopia; and the first-century
Jews were no exception. Down through the latter years of the
Old Testament period, as inspired prophets had wrestled
with their national experience of tyranny and evil, a dream of
a coming kingdom gained sharper and sharper focus in their
minds. It became clear that it would take an extraordinary

intervention on God's part to transform this present evil world into the sort of world where God's people would really feel at home. A decisive victory over the power of evil would have to be won, a victory no ordinary human being could achieve.

So they looked forward to the arrival of a supernatural deliverer, one who would be anointed like the mighty heroes of the past: a new David, but greater even than David was. They waited, in a word, for the Messiah. 'Don't worry,' said the prophets, 'things are pretty bad for us Jews in this present evil age. But soon the Messiah will step out of the wings of history. And then, at long last, the kingdom of God will begin.'

Can you imagine the shock of hope, the tremor that must have gone through the population of Galilee when Jesus, a young carpenter from Nazareth, started to wander around their towns and villages saying it had happened–the kingdom of God had come? 'Repent and believe the good news,' He said.

Oh, no doubt initially many of them were sceptical. They were not unfamiliar with megalomaniacs who indulged their manic fantasies with pretensions to be the Messiah. But this man did not just make messianic claims. He cast out demons. He healed the sick. And He taught; oh, how He taught! There was a charisma about Him that had not been seen in Israel since the days of the greatest prophets half a millenium before. There was even a rumour that He was Elijah or Jeremiah risen from the dead. That was the measure of the astonishing impact He had made.

Had He wanted to exploit the opportunity He could have set in motion a bandwagon of religious revival and political revolution that the authorities in Jerusalem and perhaps even in Rome would have been unable to stop. That word 'kingdom' resonated with all the Galilean mass's most glorious dreams, fired their most fanatical zeal and inspired their most passionate commitment. All He had to do when confronted by this vast multitude was to work a miracle or two and deliver a suitably fire-brand speech; the whole of the Galilean countryside would have erupted in volcanic enthusiasm for his Messiahship.

But the extraordinary thing is, He didn't. He told them a story instead.

Can you imagine it, this great crowd coming to Him from town after town, full of expectancy, hanging on His every word, longing to be moved with emotive oratory and impressed by supernatural power – and He sits down and tells them a story! And a bizarre, perplexing riddle of a story at that: a parable, He calls it.

Even His closest friends are utterly bewildered by His behaviour. 'What on earth are you doing, Jesus?' they asked him. 'What is this parable about?' He explained it to them: 'The knowledge of the secrets of the kingdom of God has been given to you, but to others I speak in parables, so that, "though seeing, they may not see; though hearing, they may not understand" ' (8:10).

Unpopular and controversial words. They contradict the popular view of parables as moralising stories told in picturesque imagery to give simple unsophisticated rural people an easier understanding of the message. 'On the contrary,' says Jesus, 'I speak in parables not to make it easier for people to understand, but to make it harder. Though seeing, they may not see, though hearing they may not understand.'

Whatever you make of that, it's quite clear that Jesus was not as impressed by these crowds, streaming out of all Galilee to see Him, as we might have been if we'd been there. He was not at all convinced that they were really on His wave-length. Of course He'd grown up among them. He knew perfectly well what their ideas of the kingdom of God were, as different from His own ideas as chalk from cheese. The last thing He wanted to do was to foster their mistaken notions by courting popularity with them. He hints that He feels rather as the prophet Isaiah did, when he was told to preach to a people whose hearts would be irredeemably hardened against his words. They had been so infatuated by pagan idols that could neither see nor hear that God had judicially abandoned them to spiritual blindness and deafness themselves.

It's that divine decree from Isaiah 6:9 which Jesus quotes in verse 10. The Galilean masses, according to Jesus, are in a similar spiritual state to the Jews of Isaiah's Jerusalem, incapable of comprehending the new revelation of the kingdom

of God which He had brought because their minds are preju-
dicially closed against it. Some commentators go so far as to
conclude from verse 10 that Jesus deliberately adopted a
strategy of concealment, of hiding the truth from the masses:
'He's so disillusioned with the Jewish people and convinced
that like Isaiah's Jerusalem they will reject Him in the end,
that He deliberately camouflages His message to confirm
them in their condemned state of unbelief.'

It's an arguable theory, but I think it somewhat overstates
the case. After all, if Jesus wanted to conceal His message
from the crowds altogether, why preach at all? And what are
we to make of the impassioned exhortation 'He who has ears,
let him hear' (8:8)–it sounds as if He wants an intelligent
response to His words.

I think it's closer to the truth to interpret Jesus as saying
that He uses parables as a kind of filter. Among the thousands who come out to see Him for all the wrong reasons, He
believes there are some who are genuinely open to the truth.
A tiny minority, maybe, amidst that vast spiritually deaf
multitude; but though few, they did have ears to hear. His
parables were a filter that identified those true disciples.
Those who came to Jesus looking for just a political leader, a
nationalist revolutionary or a spell-binding miracle-worker
went away disillusioned. They found, to their disappointment, just a teller of stories. But those who were drawn to
Him by some deeper magnetism, in whose hearts God's Spirit
was really working, who were being inwardly called to follow
Him–they stayed. Though they were perplexed at first just
like all the others, they were also intrigued, longing to understand what He was really getting at, sensing that somewhere
buried in the tantalising obscurity of His parables lay the
answer to the kingdom of God for which their hearts longed.
'To you,' He says to them, 'the knowledge of the secrets of
the kingdom of God has been given'.

That constitutes a fundamental lesson for us. You don't
get to grips with the message of Jesus from the safe distance
of detached curiosity. That's what Jesus is saying. Spiritual
illumination is the privilege of those who are personally committed to Him, and share the intimacy of a personal relationship. Unlike so many orators, Jesus' head was never turned

by the flattery of the crowds. He wasn't fooled by the illusion of success that big numbers conjure up. The 'mega-church' mentality with its consumer-oriented 'gospel-according-to-market-research' held no appeal for Him. He saw through it. He was perfectly content to invest Himself in just twelve men and a handful of women whom Luke names for us in verses 1–3. Provided they were real learners, real disciples, He would give the whole of Himself to such a tiny band.

Like that Galilean multitude we have streamed to Keswick. Indeed, according Matthew and Mark, that gathering took place by a lakeside! But—Why have we come? What are we expecting? Like them, perhaps, some of us have come to be entertained—we hear there are some good preachers on the menu. Perhaps some of us have come to be healed—we're troubled by some wound in our emotions or maybe in our bodies and we hope to find deliverance here. Perhaps some of us have come out of curiosity or even boredom—we've come because others were coming and we had nothing better to do.

What is your personal agenda, desire or expectation this week? Whatever it is, I strongly recommend that you put it to the back of your mind. The prior condition for receiving any blessing from Christ at all during a convention like this is a commitment to get close to Him personally. It is to disciples alone that He tells His secrets. Like that Galilean crowd, what we feel we want, and what He knows we need, may be quite incompatible. Our ideas of the kingdom of God and His ideas may be as different as chalk from cheese. If we do not want to go home, therefore, as so many of these Galileans did, disillusioned and disappointed, then our first goal must be to be open and receptive to the unexpected things that Christ will want to say to us, the unforeseen issues in our lives which He will want to address.

It's impressive and exciting for us to be part of a big crowd, to know that so many hundreds of people have gathered. I don't think He's as impressed as we are by that. He distrusts crowds. No, his blessings this week are reserved for those among us—even though they may be numbered on the fingers of His hands—who desire to be real learners, real disciples. To you, He says, the knowledge of the secrets of the kingdom of God has been given. And His parables, which He will tell us each morning at Keswick just as He told them to the Galilean crowd, are His sifting device among us–to identify who those disciples are. They're designed not only to teach us, they are designed to identify, to define, the 'teachable ones'.

Significantly, the interpretation that Jesus goes on to provide elucidates that sifting process further. Behind the pastoral imagery of the sower and the seed, He says, there is a solemn and serious truth: that only some who hear Jesus' words are ultimately blessed by Him. Tragically, many are evangelised, and yet not saved; called but not chosen.

He unfolds this cryptic story of the sower to his bewildered but intimate circle of close associates in verses 11–15. It's worth noting, before we look at that interpretation in detail, that the simple fact that Jesus does interpret His parable in this fashion explodes two of the commonest contemporary theories about parables. Some recent New Testament commentators have argued that parables should not be interpreted at all but simply retold in contemporary dress. A parable, they argue, is a rhetorical device that's designed to make an immediate impact on a live audience, so to interpret a parable is like explaining a joke–the punchline is bound to get lost in the very attempt of explaining it.

There is a profound element of truth in that. Parables are deliberately mysterious. They are intended to be elusive, there is an air of paradox and surprise which subverts the presuppositions of the listener. By drawing us into his story Jesus disarms our psychological defences so that unwelcome and unpalatable truths can strike home to our hearts. Consequently it is sometimes difficult to preach the parables in a way that recovers that original dramatic impact. Nevertheless, Jesus clearly didn't believe that it was impossible to explain parables, nor that their point was irretrievably lost in the process of trying to do so; because in Luke 8 He does so Himself.

Another major thesis commonly defended by scholars today, and also contradicted by Jesus here, is that parables are sermon illustrations, designed to make a single point and therefore never to be treated as allegories. Once again, there's an important element of truth in this. Medieval scholars sometimes allowed their imaginations to run riot in the parables seeking hidden allegorical meanings.

For example, if you study the conclusion of this parable in the Gospels of Matthew and Mark you'll find it ends slightly differently. The seed on the good ground yields varying quantities of harvest: some a hundred-fold, as here in Luke's account, but also some sixty-fold and some thirty-fold. Luke has abbreviated the story slightly. Medieval commentators eagerly seized upon that fact and engaged in all kinds of speculative ideas about the significance of the longer ending. One popular theory was that the hundred-fold yield represented martyrs who had given their lives for Christ; sixty-fold yield represented monks who had taken a vow of celibacy; and the thirty-fold yield? 'Well,' it was argued, 'obviously the thirty-fold yield represents those whose diminutive contribution to the kingdom of God is simply that of being an obedient wife!'

Clearly such a reading of Jesus' picture language is illegitimate. There's no reason at all for believing that He intends to make any comment about martyrs, monks or obedient wives in the parable of the sower. Many of the details of His parables are there not with some kind of hidden secondary meaning at all, but simply to add colour to the story.

But it will not do to insist that parables had only a single lesson to teach. For Jesus' own interpretation of this parable has decidedly allegorical features–the sower, the seed, the stony ground, the weeds–all these stand for different things. So it's clearly a mistake to draw too sharp a line between parable and allegory, or to place some arbitrary limit on how much teaching content a parable may be intended to convey.

In fact, I want to suggest to you that there are at least three vital lessons which Jesus is trying to communicate in this parable.

The central importance of the Bible for the progress of the kingdom of God

'This is the meaning of the parable: The seed is the word of God' (8:11).

We began with Jesus' gripping announcement of the kingdom of God. The powers of evil are fleeing before His face. Demons are being exorcised. Cripples are being healed. The signs of His messianic mission to transform the world are clearly apparent. But how is the world to be changed? That's the inevitable question: 'How is the kingdom to be brought in?' What strategy will Jesus employ to precipitate this decisive crisis, this decisive transformation in world history? Will He raise up an angelic army and march on Jerusalem or Rome? Will He call down supernatural fire from heaven to consume the wicked? What means does He intend to use to bring in the kingdom of God? This was a great source of debate among Jews in His day.

Indeed, it is to the answer to that very question that He refers when He speaks of the 'secrets of the kingdom of God'. He claims to bring privileged information on this vital point from the highest possible intelligence source in the universe, from heaven itself. And a clue to that secret strategy, for those who are able to penetrate the parable in which it is encoded, lies in the cipher of the seed.

Putting the evidence of all His parables and teaching together, it is clear that Jesus anticipated that the kingdom of God would come in a way hitherto unforeseen by the Jewish people – in three phases, rather than in a single apocalyptic crisis. First there would be a time of planting the kingdom, as the Messiah arrived incognito and disguised, to sow the seed of the kingdom in the hearts of a few chosen disciples. Then there would be a period of growth for the kingdom as that seed, multiplied through their testimony, fertilised many other lives until eventually the spores of the kingdom had become distributed throughout the world. And finally, He anticipated, there would be a time of reaping for the kingdom when the Messiah would return – this time amid universal public acclamation – to harvest the fruit which the seed He had sown had produced, and so bring in the full manifestation of the kingdom of which the prophets had spoken.

So the answer to that vital question, 'How is the kingdom of God to arrive?' lies in the metaphor of the seed. And what is that seed, that vital instrument by which the new age of the kingdom is sown in the very midst of the old one? Here in His first parable He leaves His disciples in no doubt. 'The seed,' He says, 'is the word.' The preaching of the gospel will be the seminal agent of change. It will germinate God's cosmic revolution. It brings in the kingdom. 'The seed is the word of God.'

It's hard to over-estimate the importance of that single brief sentence. Sadly, the church through the centuries has not always believed it. Again and again, other things have usurped the prime place the word ought to have on the Christian agenda. Once, for instance, the church revered bread and wine more than the Bible; the altar instead of the pulpit stood at the centre not only of her architecture but also of her theology.

There are still those who even today would take us back to such sacramentalist superstition if they could, but in our generation the threat to the primacy of the word has usually come from other directions. For example, social action. I'm sure many of you will know how Christians have recently pressed for a measure of political involvement. Those of you who know me will be well aware that I'm far from unsympathetic to that mood; I'm immensely supportive of it. For far too long, evangelical Christians have treated the political arena as a no-go area, as if Jesus were Lord of everywhere else except there. We have a responsibility to be the salt of the earth in council offices and in parliamentary debates, just as much as through Billy Graham crusades or overseas missions. It's good that we have learnt that in recent years.

Nevertheless, there is a danger of over-compensating for our previous neglect of social issues. We can lose touch with Jesus' priorities. The pendulum can swing to the opposite extreme. We can forget that it is through, and out of, our commitment to the word that our social concern must come. God's new society is not brought in by Act of Parliament, still less by machine gun.

Jesus was familiar with the revolutionary politics of His day. Many of the Zealot freedom-fighters came from His own home area of Galilee, but their tactics were not for Him. It was the wrong seed. He knew it. The seed is the word. A word which, when you hear it on the lips of Jesus and His

apostles, does not concern itself directly with social and economic structures. One which offers no utopian strategy for
the immediate overturn of institutional evil. A word, rather,
which is about personal repentance, personal forgiveness,
personal faith and personal discipleship. A message, as we've
already seen this morning, which is not targeted on the pol-
iticised masses but on the hearts of responsive individuals.
'He who has ears to hear, let him hear.' Notice–the third
person singular.

Superficially, no doubt, this seems a most unpromising
strategy. How can we possibly bring about the dramatic
transformation to which the prophets referred when speaking
about the kingdom of God–merely by a word? But Jesus was
convinced of it. That's why He eschewed the political path
and chose instead to be a preacher and a teacher. He was
modelling the fact that the seed is the word. So you and I do
not have to fear, in taking a gospel which is concerned
primarily with personal spiritual regeneration, that we are
not changing the world or contributing to its betterment. On
the contrary, we are changing the world far more radically
and fundamentally than any politician ever could.

For this word does not only have the power to change
social structures. It has the power to transform human hearts.
That's something vastly more impressive than you can
achieve by any number of parliamentary statutes. So don't
let's be embarrassed about giving priority to the word. Paul
wasn't. 'I am not ashamed of the gospel,' he said. 'It is the
power of God for salvation' (Rom. 1:16). Sadly, you would
not always think so when you observe the minor place given
to the Bible in many of our churches today.

Earlier I said that the sacraments once predominated in
the church's public ministry and consequently the altar
became the centrepiece of ecclesiastical architecture. It may
be significant that today pulpits are once again being pushed
into the corner–not to make room for a stone table but for an
overhead projector.

Don't misunderstand me; I use an overhead projector
myself, and I'm immensely enthusiastic about all the recent
developments in Christian worship and music–and how
grateful I am that the worship and music of the Keswick

Convention are rather more contemporary in style than when I was last here. But–just as with the issue of social involvement–there is a danger, that this bandwagon of enthusiasm for Christian music will distract us from the centrality of preaching. The seed is the word.

The same, I have to say, goes for the Signs and Wonders movement which has created such interest in the last few years. Of course, God still works miracles. And I for one am immensely grateful to those who have raised my low expectations on this matter. But Jesus could not be clearer in this parable. 'The kingdom of God,' He says, 'is not extended by the crowds observing the signs of the kingdom, but by disciples absorbing the message of the kingdom.' It is not 'He who has eyes, let him see,' but 'He who has ears, let him hear.'

I beg you, those of you who are ministers, don't let others intimidate you on this matter. Don't be diffident about putting preaching at the top of your priorities. Tell the church that you need two days or three days a week to prepare for Sunday if you're going to preach. Insist upon it. And those of you who are church members, make sure you support your minister in that. For the seed is the word.

There are, no doubt, many criticisms that could be levelled against this Keswick Convention over the years. If I'm honest, I have to say I have muttered one or two sour comments myself at times. But there is one thing this Convention has got right; it's the reason God is still blessing it and why it will continue to serve a useful purpose in this land. It puts the exposition of the word at the centre. It understands that the seed is the word. Whatever else you take back to your church this week, I beg you to take that. Take a new enthusiasm for Scripture! Learn from Jesus the central importance of the Bible to the progress of the kingdom of God.

The inevitability of failure and disappointment in Christian evangelism

'Some fell on rock . . .' (8:6).

Look again at how He tells the story. It's not how a

teacher of homiletics in one of our very modern Bible colleges would have told it. Jesus here describes one homogeneous sowing and four different soils. If our modern expert in the science of communication were to tell the parable, it would undoubtedly be the other way round. He would speak of one homogeneous soil and four different sowers. The first sower sowed the seed one way, but it didn't work; the second sower used a different tactic but that was no good either; the third tried another but still had no success; and then finally along came the sower who had read his church growth handbook, done his sociological analysis, got his communication technique perfected – and he got a harvest. Well done, that preacher.

'No!' says Jesus. 'That's not the way it is. Success or failure of the seed of the word is not a function of the sower's technique at all.' On the contrary, the seed is sown in what seems like an artless, almost wasteful way that demands no skill at all. It's just scattered. For it is not the function of the sower to change one soil into another. It is rather, says Jesus, a function of the seed to highlight the intrinsic fertility or infertility of the soil.

Again, don't misunderstand me. No doubt there are plenty of things we can all learn usefully about evangelistic methodology. We could all be more effective sowers of the word, and I'm sure Jesus, by shaping the story as He does, isn't ruling out the possibility of our improving ourselves in that way. But we deceive ourselves if we think that the conversion of men and women is something that lies in our hands, to be achieved if only we can discover the right approach. Not so! The preaching of the word is not intended to be an exercise in human manipulation. The preaching of the word, in Jesus' mind, is a demonstration of divine grace. In the preaching event, it is the quality of the soil, not the expertise of the sower, that is primarily displayed.

Of course we don't like that. For a start, it robs us of our best excuse for our rejection of the gospel – namely, that the preacher was no good. What's more, it deflates the evangelist's pride terribly, doesn't it? For it means that the best and most faithful preacher will know failure and disappointment. Even more mortifying, it means that the worst and most ill-disciplined preacher may well know success and blessing. For as Paul himself says, the sower and the waterer are nothing. It is only God who gives the growth (see 1 Cor. 3:7).

This is no excuse, of course, for a slap-dash, negligent attitude among those of us who are evangelists or preachers. We shall answer to God for the way we use our talents, but the fact is, at the end of the day, whether our preaching is technically good or bad, we are all of us unprofitable servants—useless. It is the soil that makes the difference. Spiritual fertility does not lie in our gift. Would that it did! How successful we would manage to be, if it did! But because it doesn't we must expect three categories of disappointment.

Those along the path
'...The ones who hear, and then the devil comes and takes away the word from their hearts...' (8:12). Jesus is candid here about the prolific waste of effort which evangelism will often seem to be. As He speaks He's looking out at that vast crowd, one we'd be delighted to see gather into our churches on a Sunday morning. And many of us would be tempted, I'm sure, to label many or even all of these casual adherents to Jesus as immediate converts. After all, the mere fact that they were coming to Him from their homes surely indicates response of a sort, doesn't it? But Jesus is not so easily convinced. 'No,' He says, 'this is a very mixed multitude I see. Some of these people who have come out to hear me quite obviously are hardened against My word.' That hardening may come from intellectual pride—'He doesn't seriously expect me to believe that, does He?'; from moral obstinacy—'There's no way I'm going to stop doing that, just because He says so'; from self-righteousness—'Me, a sinner? How dare He!'; or it may be simply the hardening of bored indifference—'Yeah, well guess this isn't my scene, man, I'm into yoga.'

They may have come to hear His word, but it rolled off them like water off a duck's back. Their hearts were coated in spiritual teflon so nothing stuck. Perhaps they thought they were being clever, sophisticated, not taken in by all this kingdom-of-God nonsense. But notice the one whom Jesus identifies silently, secretly campaigning behind this defiant,

cynical attitude. 'The devil comes and takes away the word so
they can't believe and be saved,' He says.

You want to know where the devil is this morning? He's
right here, sitting on our shoulders. He's always there when
the word is being exposed to people, because he knows the
seed is the word even if others don't. He'll use every psychological trick in the book to discredit it and distract our attention from it. And in the case of these hardened hearts, says
Jesus, he succeeds; and there's nothing the preacher can do
to stop him succeeding. It's just the sort of soil they are.
What preacher doesn't know the disappointment that comes
from facing up to the reality of hardened hearts? Some of us
have to come to terms with it within our own families, and
that is even more heart-breaking.

Would that that were the end of the disappointment. But
Jesus says no, there's more.

Those on the rock
'... The ones who receive the word with joy when they hear
it, but they have no root' (8:13). Others in the crowd represent only a superficial decision, an initial enthusiasm that
doesn't last. Their response to the word is all emotion, a kind
of animal excitement that you get from being part of a big
crowd or the kind of warm fuzzies that you get from watching
a sentimental movie. They receive the word with joy, says
Jesus, but then circumstances change, the adrenalin subsides,
the intoxication of the moment fades. Perhaps they begin to
feel cheated. 'They told me Christianity made you feel
happy–well, I don't. They told me Christianity would give
me friends–well, I haven't got any. It must have been just an
adolescent phase I went through, just a flash in the pan. I'm
not going to be a Christian any longer.'

They have no root. They believe for a while, but in the
time of testing they apostasise, says Jesus. Again, who hasn't
seen it in our churches? They come in, but its a five-minute
wonder. For a while they're wonderful Christians. They go
through all the baptismal classes, the confirmation classes,
they are involved in everything. And then six months later
they're nowhere to be seen. Who hasn't seen it?

And would that that were the end of the disappointment.
But no. Jesus says there's more to come.

Those among thorns

'...Those who hear, but as they go on their way they are choked...and they do not mature' (8:14). There are still others who turn out to be distracted disciples. Again, there's an enthusiastic initial response. But unlike the case of the superficial decision, these people do not seem to renege on their commitment to Jesus altogether. They retain some kind of Christian identity. They don't fall away in that sense. But as time goes on, Christ becomes less and less significant in their lives. The couch-grass of rival interests clogs their energies. The bindweed of materialism and worldliness saps all those early hopes of spirituality.

In their youth, perhaps, it is educational goals, sporting achievement or sexual attraction that's responsible for this diversion of interest. In mid-life it's financial stress, family responsibilities, career ambition. In old age it's the pre-occupation with health, or the garden or the grandchildren. Whatever stage in life we're at there are dozens of such distractions. 'As they go on their way,' says Jesus, 'they are choked by life's worries, riches and pleasures.' The result is they do not mature. They're in a state of arrested spiritual development. They call themselves Christian but it's really very, very nominal.

Do we not see in our churches dozens, hundreds, thousands of such nominal Christians? Make no mistake about it, evangelism is full of discouragement. No matter how gifted we may be, no matter how well trained, no matter how disciplined in our studies, no matter how passionate in our hearts, no matter how personally devoted to Christ–every evangelist has to come to terms with failure and disappointment on a huge scale. Many will hear and never return. Others will rush to make a decision for Christ and later be nowhere to be found. Still others will sit in the pew week after week like passengers on a train and never stir a muscle. Jesus found it so, Paul found it so, Whitefield found it so, Spurgeon found it so, Dr Lloyd-Jones found it so, Dr Billy Graham finds it so, every preacher and evangelist on this platform finds it so. And if you're engaged in any ministry of the word, whether as a preacher, evangelist, Bible class leader or missionary or whatever else, you will find it so. Why should you be surprised that you know failure and disappointment? Jesus said we would. There's only one comfort for the soul amidst all this sad tale of wasted effort.

Those on good soil
'Still other seed fell on good soil. It came up and yielded a crop, a hundred times more than was sown' (8:8). If you're feeling downcast because your ministry seems to be unproductive and sterile, don't despair. You haven't got it wrong. The seed is the word. It is the only way to increase the kingdom. And increase it will. Jesus assures us of that in spite of all these frustrating losses and wasted efforts, the farmer will have a splendid crop at the end of the day.

> God's word, for all their craft and force,
> One moment will not linger:
> But, in spite of hell, shall have its course:
> 'Tis written by His finger.
>
> (Martin Luther)

But that brings me to the final lesson I want you to learn from our passage.

The enduring evidence that distinguishes a true Christian conversion

'... Those with a noble and good heart, who hear the word, retain it, and by persevering produce a crop' (8:15). Commentators disagree about how many of these four soils may represent hope of salvation. All agree that the seed sown along the path certainly does not. The text itself excludes such a possibility. They cannot believe and be saved, says Jesus of those hardened hearts.

But there are many who would like to argue that the other three soils, though differing in the degree of spirituality which they represent, all nevertheless represent a saving response to the gospel. 'After all,' they say, 'the seed sown among the stones and among the weeds still germinates, doesn't it? The word is received, a decision for Christ is made, the path of discipleship is at least begun. Such responsive individuals are surely born again,' they say, 'and are therefore assured of eternal life even if their lack of sustained commitment and spiritual growth forfeits their heavenly rewards. It can't, surely, forfeit heaven itself.'

Well, I have to tell you that I am sorely troubled by that kind of interpretation. I'm not at all convinced that Jesus, or the New Testament generally, would be so generous. What, I ask myself about Jesus' searching words in the Sermon on the Mount about those nominal disciples who had made a verbal profession? 'Not everyone who says to me, "Lord, Lord," will enter the kingdom, but only those who do the will of my Father who is in heaven. Many will say to me on that day, "Lord, Lord..." [and] I will tell them plainly, "I never knew you. Away from me!" ' (Matt. 7:21–23). Or what about that solemn picture of the vine He gives us in the Gospel of John? 'The branch,' he says, 'which does not bear fruit is cut off, and thrown into the fire' (see John 15:5). What about that solemn warning to apostates in the letter to the Hebrews, 6:4–6? 'Land that produces thorns and thistles is worthless,' says the writer, 'in the end it will be burned' (Heb. 6:8). What about that frightening admonition of the risen Christ to those half-hearted so-called believers in the church at Laodicea (Rev. 3:16)?

It is surely the implication of this parable that for Jesus the only adequate response to the word was one that issued in an enduring spiritual productivity. Nothing less would do. John McArthur put it very well in a book on this subject that I warmly commend to you, *The Gospel According To Jesus*.[1]

> Fruit-bearing is the whole point of agriculture. In the harvest weedy soil offers no more hope than does the hard road or the shallow ground. All are equally worthless for all are equally fruitless. Fruit-bearing is the whole point of agriculture and it is also the ultimate test, then, of salvation.

When we assess the results of our evangelism we must face the fact that initial professions of faith are a misleading statistic. It is the long-term productivity, not the short-term enthusiasm that results from evangelism that really cheers the heart of Christ.

I say this because it seems to me that one of our biggest problems in the church today, on both sides of the Atlantic, is that there is abroad amongst us what I sometimes call the 'fire-insurance' definition of faith. It's propagated by hundreds of well-meaning Christians, but it is a dangerous misrepresentation of the truth in my view because it says this: 'Decide for Jesus now, make a commitment to Jesus right now; because once you've made that response, you have eternal life, and you must never, never doubt it. By this simple step of faith you have guaranteed for yourself admission to heaven absolutely and irrevocably.'

It sounds like authentic gospel preaching, and it can very nearly be so; but it can also be a distortion of New Testament Christianity. For as a result of that kind of initial counselling many thousands of professing Christians think they can live the rest of their life as they please. They are completely morally complacent. They may surrender to all kinds of moral or spiritual collapse in their later lives, and yet insist that when the last curtain goes down, they will be all right. Because all those years ago they were counselled by an evangelist who told them that, since they had made a decision for Christ, they had eternal life and they must never doubt it. They got their fire insurance that night, they paid a single lifetime premium.

I do not believe that's a doctrine of assurance which the New Testament will countenance. The New Testament insists that assurance of eternal salvation is only valid if it is supported by the clear evidence of spiritual growth and productivity. That doesn't mean a salvation by works. But it does mean that the only reliable evidence of salvation is goodness.

It is those who by persevering produce a crop, who are secure, says Jesus. Perseverance is the hallmark of the truly converted man or woman. There is no encouragement here to spiritual complacency on the part of fruitless branches. To be frank, it is the unwillingness of some of us preachers and evangelists to face up to the tough implications of this parable of the sower that has led, over the last hundred years, to many destructive doctrinal aberrations.

We want, understandably, to affirm the eternal salvation of everybody who has made any kind of response to the gospel whatsoever, no matter how short-lived or ineffectual. And so we find ways of giving assurance to backsliders and apostates and nominal believers. Sometimes we say, 'They've been justified, they've just not been sanctified yet'; sometimes, 'They have taken Jesus as their saviour, but they've not taken Him as their lord yet'; sometimes 'They've been born again by the Spirit, but they've not yet been filled with the Spirit'; sometimes 'Oh well, they've had their first blessing, but they haven't had their second blessing yet.'

I have to tell you, I don't find such a two-stage theory of salvation offered by the apostles in the New Testament. The reason we offer it is because we are not prepared to say of this person, 'Yes, he said he was a convert, but you can tell from his life now that he isn't. Yes, he made a decision for Christ, but he was never really born again.'

We don't want to say that, but Jesus will. Preachers of an earlier generation were less shy. There was no 'fire insurance' definition of faith for them. Charles Spurgeon, walking to his church in London, once came across a drunk clinging to a lamp-post. 'I'm one of your converts, Mr Spurgeon,' said the drunk. 'You may well be one of my converts,' replied Spurgeon, 'but you're certainly not one of God's converts, or you wouldn't be in this condition.'

You see, the seed of the word, when it is savingly received, doesn't just produce a temporary effect. It produces enduring change. True faith is not just an ephemeral whim in the emotional excitement of an evangelistic meeting. It's not just a nominal nod of the head in the direction of the altar when the Creed is repeated on Sunday evening. True faith is a deliberate and determined pledge of the heart to a faithfulness and an obedience to Christ and His word, which perseveres through trials and opposition and sustains its growth life-long. I'm not saying Christians don't have setbacks; of course they do. But they endure. And it is only those who endure to the end who are saved.

There are such things as abortive conversion experiences. There is Judas among the Twelve, there is Ananias and Sapphira among the congregation. That's why the New Testament exhorts us: 'See to it, brothers, that none of you has a sinful, unbelieving heart that turns away from the living God...We have come to share in Christ if we hold firmly till the end the confidence we had at first' (Heb. 3:12,14).

What sort of hearing have you engaged in this morning?

Was it the hearing of the seed along the path–you heard, but you haven't listened? Have we heard only with our emotions—is it all going to evaporate away when we get out in that so-called 'real world?' Have we heard just with our minds, enthused, perhaps, with some ideas that seem new, but they're all going to be choked off next week when it's a choice between Christ or our bank account?

Or have we heard with our whole being; not just with ears or minds, but with heart and will and soul, unconditionally and absolutely responding to the claim of this sovereign word, which is the seed of the kingdom?

The kingdom of God begins in our lives when God's rule begins in our lives. And how does God assert his rule in our lives? It is by the obedient attention we pay to what he says.

1. John McArthur, *The Gospel According to Jesus: Salvation Without Obedience?* (USA: Zondervan, 1988).

2. The Meaning of Love:
(Luke 10:25–37)

Judging by the frequency with which the word is celebrated in the Top Twenty, it's quite clear that for many the single answer to the world's troubles is 'love'. And it's not difficult to agree with sentiments like that when you observe what hate does on the world's stage; all the misery it inflicts, the violence it perpetrates, the broken homes, communities, lives and hearts for which it is responsible. It's almost platitudinous to say, in the words of that sixties song of John Lennon, 'All you need is love.' The problem is it's one thing to sing about it, and another thing altogether to do it, isn't it?

We all know love could bring reconciliation in Northern Ireland; it could solve the tensions of the Middle East; it could heal the warring factions of South Africa. In short, we all know that love could make the whole world go round a great deal more smoothly. The trouble is, we just don't seem to be able to inject enough of this miracle-working moral lubricant into the world's bearings.

Everyone gives assent in principle to the importance of love. But one despairs of finding any out of all the divided peoples of our globe where it is actually being demonstrated. This is nothing new, of course. Two thousand years ago, the thoughtful scribes of Judea had already identified the primary importance of love from their studies of the Bible. But in their case, too, there was a disappointing performance-gap between theory and practice. And Jesus tells a classic story to impress that very point on one learned rabbi with whom he discusses the matter. We're going to look at it together under three headings: the theory of love, the practice of love, and the challenge of love.

The theory of love (10:25–28)

Any of you who've tried your hand at public debate will be familiar with the kind of person who stands up during question time, not with the aim of furthering serious discussion, but simply in order to make a fool of the speaker. I remember when I was at school we had a mock general election, when various senior scholars stood as candidates for the major political parties. I was going through my anarchist phase at that time, so I declined to stand for office myself. But I did gain, I remember, immense satisfaction instead by interrupting every campaign speech I could by demanding in a loud voice, 'What about pig-rearing in the Shetland Islands?' None of the adolescent parliamentarians at my school, I discovered, had given much thought to this serious question. And not a few were reduced to total confusion by being asked to comment on it.

These days, unfortunately, I tend to be on the other end of such subversive tactics. In fact, any preacher who accepts speaking engagements at schools with a preponderance of A-level students quickly forms a list of old chestnuts of this sort. Who was Cain's wife? That's a good one. Did Noah have polar bears in the Ark? That's another. One soon learns that people who ask questions like this don't really want an answer, they just want to score points in an intellectual sparring match. It was Martin Luther who executed the most sardonic parry to such an inquiry. He was asked by one garrulous sceptic once, 'What was God doing before He made the world?' To which Luther is reputed to have replied, 'Making hell for people who ask stupid questions like that.'

When we read the Gospels we discover that Jesus had to cope with a good many such insincere inquirers. Again and again the theologians of His day tried to trap Him into making some injudicious comment by which He could be discredited. But it's interesting to observe the way that Jesus refused to be drawn into sterile, speculative arguments. He was, in fact, the master of turning such questions back on the interrogator.

In these verses before us we find a classic example of Him handling just such a would-be controversialist; an expert in the law, Luke calls him, or – as we would call him today – an Old Testament scholar. He raises a query and on the surface it sounds guileless enough. Indeed, the man seems to hold Jesus in considerable esteem because he stands to put his question and addresses Him respectfully as 'Teacher'. What's more the enquiry itself appears, superficially at any rate, to be rather promising. 'Teacher,' he says, 'what must I do to inherit eternal life?' But in order that we should not be misled, Luke tells us his inner motive was rather more disappointing. He stood up, he tells us, to put Jesus to the test.

So this man was not a genuine seeker after spiritual illumination. He was one more of those hostile inquisitors from the Jewish establishment who were looking for an opportunity to examine Jesus' theological credentials and, if possible, expose His theological incompetence. No doubt he hoped that Jesus would make some wild messianic claim or utter some heretical statement which could be taken down and used as evidence later against Him.

But if so, he was frustrated. For instead of volunteering some theological novelty for him to seize upon, Jesus invited the man to answer his own question from the Old Testament which he knew so well. 'What's written in the law?' He said. 'How do you read it?' And the man was, not surprisingly, only too willing to exhibit the fruits of his biblical research. 'Love the Lord your God,' he says, 'and your neighbour as yourself.'

'You've answered correctly,' Jesus replied.

You may be a little surprised to find this man summarising the Old Testament law in those terms. For Jesus himself, when asked on another occasion to identify the most important commandment in the Bible could do no better than to cite precisely the same two texts which this scribe quotes here – Deuteronomy 6:5 and Leviticus 19:18. 'Love God. Love your neighbour. The entire moral teaching of the Bible,' He said, 'hinges on these two pivotal imperatives.'

So it says much, does it not, for the profundity of this

scribe's reflection on Biblical ethics, that he had come inde-
pendently to exactly the same conclusion as Jesus on this
point?

Well–actually, no. It probably indicates nothing of the
sort. Almost certainly, the fact that the lawyer fastens here
on the same two Old Testament quotations as Jesus implies
rather that, contrary perhaps to what many of us assume,
Jesus was not the first to link those two Old Testament
commandments or to distil out of them the kernel of God's
moral requirement. It seems much more likely that this
scribe's answer represented the conventional wisdom of the
rabbis of Jesus' day. If you had asked any of them, 'What's
the essence of the law, what is the cardinal virtue?' they
would have all answered with one voice, 'Love God and love
your neighbour.'

The apostle Paul is perhaps echoing his own recollection
of that commonplace rabbinical maxim when he tells us in
Romans: 'Love is the fulfilment of the law' (Rom. 13:10).
And that being so, I suspect this Old Testament expert may
have been a little nonplussed when Jesus, this Galilean with
such a reputation for radical ideas, applauds his very traditional answer and agrees with its uncontroversial orthodoxy.
'You've answered correctly,' Jesus replies. 'Do this, and you
will live.'

Perhaps some of us too are a little disturbed that Jesus
should seem to endorse this man's ideas so uncritically.
Surely the whole point about Jesus was that He had something new to say about the way to eternal life, something
fundamentally contradictory to the Judaism in which this
man had grown up. But by replying to him in such a flattering
and supportive fashion it sounds for all the world as if Jesus
wants to deny any revolutionary or innovative element in His
proclamation of the kingdom of God.

Well, if that's how you're tempted to react to verse 28, I
have to tell you that I think you're making two mistakes.

Firstly, you're misunderstanding the teaching of Jesus.
The New Testament never abrogates the moral demands of
the Old Testament law. On the contrary, it everywhere insists
that the new covenant people of God can be identified by the
obedience to that moral law which the Holy Spirit works into

their lives. When Jesus in verse 28 says 'Do this and you will live,' He's not implying that loving deeds can earn heaven for us; but He is most certainly confirming that loving deeds are the infallible mark of a heaven-bound personality.

This is exactly the conclusion we drew from the parable of the sower yesterday: that you can tell fertile ground which has received the seed of the word by the moral fruit of obedience to that word which it bears. Some of you felt that when I raised doubts about whether the stony or the thorny ground represented any hope of salvation, I was thereby demanding sinless perfection of Christians or denying the eternal security of the believer. Let me emphasise, I wasn't arguing for either of those things.

I was simply insisting upon that doctrine of assurance which is confirmed by the repeated testimony of the Bible, that the people of God must be morally distinguishable from the world. We therefore may only claim to be members of the people of God if there is clear evidence of moral obedience to God's word in our lives. The New Testament does not demand sinless perfection of Christians; but it most certainly demands moral change. It does not teach that any true believer can perish; but it certainly doesn't give eternal security to unrepentant back-sliders. On the contrary, it insists that if we want to make our calling and election sure, then we must add virtue to our faith. 'It is only,' says Peter, 'as we add to our faith virtue, as we show in the quality of our lives that we are doing those things which holiness demands, that we may rest assured that we shall never fall' (see 1 Peter 1:5–11).

It's against that background, I suggest, that we should understand Jesus' answer to this scribe. The man was effectively asking, 'How can I be certain I belong to the people of God, that I'm one of those who'll inherit the messianic kingdom of God when it arrives?' Jesus' answer is no revolutionary new concept. It is in Deuteronomy just as it is in John. It is in Leviticus just as it is in Romans. We know that we have passed from death to life because we love. Love is the timeless divine requirement. Without it we shall not enter heaven, for heaven is a world of love, and he who hates is still on the path of destruction.

This lawyer, you see, answered better than he knew. People who are going to heaven do love God and their neighbour. The law written on tablets of stone by Moses in the Old Testament, which this man knew so well, is the same moral law which is written on the tablets of the human heart by the Holy Spirit of the New Testament which Jesus had come to inaugurate. As Christ Himself said, 'I haven't come to abolish the law, but to fulfil it.' And love is the fulfilment of the law. In that sense, Jesus is saying nothing at all contradictory to the general tenor of the New Testament when He says, 'Do this, and you will live.'

But I imagine some of you will still not be satisfied with that. You'll object further. 'Oh, that may be so,' you will say. 'Moral obedience is the evidence of a spiritually renewed personality. We all know that. But it is certain that this scribe did not have such a New Testament theological perspective on things. It's quite clear he was spiritually astray, for just look at the way he frames his initial question. 'What shall I *do* to inherit eternal life?' Didn't he see the contradiction in his own words? Nobody inherits anything by *doing* things, do they? An inheritance is something you receive by virtue of a relationship, not of an achievement.'

Clearly, like many Jews of this period and many nominal Christians of today, this man thought of eternal life as something purchased by your own works of piety rather than given freely by God's grace. It was not a matter of 'What has God done for me,' but rather of 'What must I do for God?' He didn't see love of God and neighbour as the evidential fruit which the Holy Spirit produced in the lives of those who had received eternal life. He saw it merely as the moral duty which he, by his own unaided efforts, had to perform in order to gain eternal life as a divine reward. That was how his mind worked.

Surely Jesus should have corrected that legalistic self-righteousness underlying the scribe's words? But instead in verse 28 Jesus seems to almost pat the man on the back and compliment him on his sound approach. 'Do this and you shall live.'

'That's not the right answer, Jesus—not for this man! You should have pointed him to faith, not to works, just as Paul does in the letter of the Galatians.' If that's your response, it brings me to the second mistake I think you may be making. Besides perhaps misunderstanding the teaching of Jesus, you may also be underestimating his pastoral wisdom.

Think for a moment about the kind of man this expert in the law was. A professional Bible student; a man who had memorised Genesis to Deuteronomy, who had participated in seminar after seminar of learned debate, sharpening his arguments, clarifying his finer points. A man who had not only examined countless real legal cases but had dreamed up thousands of imaginary ones, so that he could feel absolutely sure there was no conceivable ethical problem upon which he could not pronounce an authoritative opinion. In short, here was a man with all the answers. Such a person neither needs nor wants theological instruction. That wasn't why he came to Jesus. He had a mind stuffed to the brim with theological instruction, and given half a chance would be only too delighted to parade it for everybody's benefit.

Debate with a person like that, I would suggest, is a pointless exercise. It might entertain the crowd, but it's most unlikely to change his mind in any way. Indeed the philosopher Karl Popper may have been right when he argued that such debate only serves to cement the protagonists ever more securely in their rival positions. Even if Jesus had succeeded in confuting the scribe's theology by such means, He would not have succeeded in converting his soul. He would have won the argument but not the man.

This man needed not to be taught but humbled. That first-person 'What must *I* do' betrayed altogether too much self-confidence. He really thought he could love God and neighbour. That was his most fundamental error; not his legalistic theology, but his moral complacency. The only way this man could be really helped was by puncturing that confident veneer of smug self-righteousness with a little bit of old-fashioned conviction of sin.

But as every counsellor knows, conviction of sin cannot be taught by lecturing people on the subject. When you're seeking to lead a person along the path to repentance, indirect methods are often far more effective than confrontational ones. Jesus, the master psychiatrist, knows that. He would

show this man the inadequacy of his theology of good works.
But not by scoring a victory over him in theoretical debate;
rather, by touching his conscience with a very practical story.

And that brings us to our second parable.

The practice of love (10:29–35)

It's clear from verse 29 that the lawyer felt that in spite of
Jesus' apparently complimentary response he had, nevertheless, somehow been defeated. Perhaps there had been just an
edge to Jesus' tone when He said, 'Do this, and you will
live'–as if to imply 'but you don't really love like this, do
you?' That certainly seems to be the implication of Luke's
observation, that the man sensed some need to 'justify himself', that is to put himself in the right. The moral challenge
of Jesus' words had left him on the defensive. Though
nothing explicitly disapproving had been said, he unaccountably felt as though he had been rebuked.

But isn't that how we all feel when someone challenges us
with the command to love? G. K. Chesterton once said that
Christianity had not been tried and found wanting; it had
been found difficult and left untried. That's about the size of
it. As we said earlier, everybody agrees that 'Love your
neighbour' is fine in theory, but when it comes to practice we
find ourselves embarrassed by the unconditional demands
such a rule makes upon our lives. Almost unconsciously, we
seek to ease the pressure on our consciences, to convince
ourselves that in spite of that nagging uncomfortable feeling
of self-reproach, we do love our neighbour as ourselves–
don't we?

There are two classic ways in which we habitually seek to
achieve this sense of self-justification. And it's the genius of
Jesus' parable that it unmasks the essential hypocrisy in both
of them.

The 'I don't do anybody any harm' technique

This first technique is quite simple. You turn God's positive
command into a negative prohibition. 'Love your neighbour'
is transformed into 'Don't do anybody any harm'. Such passive righteousness is far easier to handle. We can comfort
ourselves, since we haven't stolen from, murdered or slan-

dered our neighbour, that we have thereby succeeded in loving him or her. That was clearly the attitude of the priest and the Levite in Jesus' story. I've no doubt these two clergymen were well able to rationalise their decision to pass by on the other side in any number of ways. Just like this lawyer, they could justify themselves.

To begin with they could claim that it would be foolish to stop. This injured man might have been a decoy to trap naive travellers who let their emotions get the better of their common sense. Then they could argue that it would have been unbiblical for them to stop: we are told that the man was 'half-dead'—that is, unconscious. For all they knew, he might have been fully dead. If so, then the ceremonial law of the Old Testament forbade any member of the temple staff to go within six feet of him. If either of these clergymen had gone over to investigate, only to find they were dealing with a corpse, they would have become ritually defiled. And that would have meant not only going through an irksome procedure of ceremonial cleansing, but of being ruled unfit to carry out their liturgical duties for a considerable period of time to everybody's inconvenience and their considerable embarrassment.

But the chief reason they were able to defend their neglect of this injured man was because their interpretation of the law of love did not require them to do anything for him. A passive righteousness that simply refrained from inflicting actual harm on other people was all that was demanded, so far as they were concerned. They hadn't beaten the poor fellow up, had they? Therefore they were not responsible; therefore they didn't have to get involved. That was how their minds worked. Theirs was an ethic which took no account at all of sins of omission, and which could therefore ignore the man without suffering the slightest pang of guilt. 'Why,' they might have said to themselves as they continued down the road, 'he might not have even been a Jew anyway!'

And that brings us to the second strategy.

The 'Charity begins at home' technique
This technique involves setting limits on the extent of the application of God's command to love. It restricts the operation of that command to a particular group of people who

are regarded as the exclusive recipients of the love of which it speaks.

'Who is my neighbour?' our scribe asks–the implication being that some people are my neighbour and some people aren't. He would have taken it for granted that 'Love your neighbour' meant 'Love your fellow Jew'. No rabbi of the day would have suggested anything else. The question in his mind was probably, 'Does that include Gentile converts to Judaism?'; because we know that the rabbis were divided on that issue in Jesus' day. Perhaps he thought that by getting Jesus' opinion on that controversy he could generate the academic debate he was seeking. But he can scarcely have been ready for the bombshell that would fall at the very centre of Jesus' story in reply to this technical query.

To understand the emotional impact of verses 33–34 on Jesus' original audience, one needs somehow got to get inside the feelings of contempt which Jews entertained towards Samaritans in the first century. The reasons for that contempt we needn't go into. Like all ethnophobia, it was thoroughly irrational. But seldom in the history of the world, I suspect, has there been a racist prejudice that was quite so extreme in the intensity of its mutual loathing.

Unfortunately, this dimension of the story is lost on us. We are so familiar with this parable that the very word 'Samaritan' for us has connotations of benevolence. We all know Samaritans are good. They are those good people who sit on the end of telephones all night long, waiting to counsel potential suicides. But such philanthropic associations were quite foreign to the first-century Jewish mind. On the contrary, in their culture there was no such thing as a 'good' Samaritan. As the American cavalry used to say of the Apaches, the only good Samaritan was a dead Samaritan. And that's no exaggeration. Samaritans were publicly cursed in the synagogues. Petitions were daily offered begging God to deny them any participation in eternal life. Many rabbis even said that a Jewish beggar should refuse alms from a Samaritan because their very money was contaminated. It wasn't a case of their being no love lost between these two groups. There was no love to lose.

Jesus could not possibly have chosen a hero more offensive to the sensitivities of His audience. And it is not going too far to suggest that He displayed considerable physical courage in doing so. It would be like siding with a black at an Afrikaner brotherhood meeting in Johannesburg. Or like praising a UDR soldier in a Catholic pub in Belfast. If Jesus had made it a Jew helping a Jew it would have been acceptable. Even a Jew helping a Samaritan might have been tolerable. Some, I'm sure, would have applauded if He'd made His story a piece of anti-clerical propaganda, with the Jewish layman showing up the hypocrisy of these two members of the priesthood. But to suggest that two pillars of the Jewish establishment should be morally outclassed by this mongrel heretic—why, it would have stung every Jewish patriot into hostile indignation! Yet that was exactly Jesus' suggestion.

At every step in the narrative, He makes the Samaritan fulfil the duty of love so conspicuously neglected by the priest and the Levite. Their hearts had been cold and calculating, but his burns with an extravagant compassion. Their oil and wine remains undefiled in their saddle bags, ready, no doubt, for later use in temple ritual. But his becomes a soothing and antiseptic balm to treat the man's wounds. They stay securely seated on their beasts, ready to gallop off should the man's prone body prove to be a decoy. He bravely dismounts, risking possible ambush, and walks the rest of the way to Jericho with the injured man slumped in his own saddle. They kept their money safe in their purse, congratulating themselves, no doubt, on that ten percent tithe they had just paid up in the capital. But he freely sacrifices a month's wages or more in order to secure the nursing care this man would need to make a full recovery.

And note very carefully: all this he did in complete ignorance of the man's racial identity. That is the significance, you see, of Jesus' observation that this man was unconscious and stripped naked. All the normal means by which the ethnic identity of somebody could be established in the Middle East—his dialect and manner of dress—were missing. The Samaritan encounters this victim of criminal violence simply as an anonymous human being. Jew, Gentile, fellow Samaritan—he can't know which. Yet he cares for him. He rescues him. He provides sacrificially for his future welfare.

The implication is clear, and Jesus pulls no punches in pointing it out.

The challenge of love (10:36–37)

You can see the lawyer swallowing hard, can't you, as Jesus forces him to answer his own question again? He can't bring himself to say, 'the Samaritan', for that hated word would have stuck in his throat. On the other hand, he can't deny the moral force of the story he's heard. So he replies with embarrassed circumlocution, 'the one who had mercy on him'.

There must have been a glimmer of a smile on Jesus' lips as He observes his discomfiture. This man who had come for a sparring match now finds himself, not just defeated, but convicted. Jesus told him, 'Go and do likewise.' And surely in those two imperatives 'go' and 'do' Jesus unmasks the hypocrisy not only of his original enquirer but also of us all. It is so easy, isn't it, to engage in high-sounding generalisations about loving people? But this masterpiece of a parable grounds the practical implications of that moral theory in real life. How much are you really prepared to 'go and do, for love of neighbour's sake?' it asks.

How much value does love place on a human being? The legalist wants to calculate that sum in very precise terms, so that he might know the limit of his moral duty. 'If I do this much, I have loved.' The effect of that kind of moral computation is to turn love into a very tepid thing; a vague, generalised benevolence which cannot possibly express the infinite preciousness of a human individual at all. We put our subscription in the famine relief fund, we buy our flag from the street collector, and we say, 'There! We've done it. We've loved our neighbour. We've obeyed the command.'

'Rubbish,' says Jesus. 'You haven't even begun yet.' Have you noticed how very careful God is to express His command in the singular? 'You shall love your neighbour.' Love cannot be satisfied with charitable generalities. Says Charlie Brown indignantly in the Peanuts cartoon: 'Of course I love the human race, I just can't stand Lucy.' But Lucy is the measure of love.

Jesus is here concerned to show us that love requires an intensity of preoccupation with an individual. That is love's test. For the human race, we can do very little; that's why it's so easy to say we love them. But there is no limit at all to the lengths to which we might go in showing generosity to the specific needy individual who happens to cross our path, if we value them highly enough.

I'm not denying that the world today is in such great need that bureaucratic charity is necessary. I know hungry people have to become statistics on pieces of paper that are passed around desks and offices and through computer memory-banks. But be sure of this. That kind of de-personalised care cannot possibly fulfil our obligation to love as God sees it. Real neighbour-love can only flow in the context of a one-to-one, I-thou relationship. For only in such a relationship can the extravagance of love find practical expression.

Don't you remember, in John 12, Judas's irritation when Mary of Bethany, overcome with devotion to the Lord, poured that valuable jar of perfumed ointment at His feet? 'Why wasn't this ointment sold for 300 denarii and the money given to the poor?' Notice–'the poor'. Judas characteristically thought in such categories. Nice, safe, plural, generalised, collective nouns. 'The poor'. But Mary didn't think that way at all. For her, it was Jesus, an individual, a person she loved and would do anything for. Of course it was extravagant. But love is extravagant. In vain do you tell the lover, when he looks in the jeweller's window, 'You can't possibly afford that one.' Love sweeps such economic considerations aside. It goes the extra mile, it offers the cloak as well as the coat, it even turns the other cheek. To cold calculating Judas this was unintelligible and wasteful. But Mary knew that love could not limit itself by degrees. Love is not interested in calculating 'What is the least I can do to fulfil my duty?' It sets such enormous value on a human individual that it must sacrifice anything on their behalf. Until it has been so extravagant, it is frustrated and unexpressed.

'Go and do likewise,' says Jesus. 'Next time, Mr Lawyer, you see somebody whom it lies in your power to help, remember My story of the Good Samaritan and go and do likewise. Then you'll know what loving your neighbour's all about.'

Must He not say something similar to us? Has He not at a single stroke exposed the fallaciousness of all those clever excuses and rationalisations we use? 'I don't do anybody any harm.' What sort of neighbour-love is that? Such a love would have left this poor man to perish, and congratulated itself on its sound judgement. 'Charity begins at home.' What sort of neighbour-love is that? Had the noble Samaritan himself been the victim in question, such a love would have left him to die and congratulated itself on its moral discrimination.

Jesus' story dramatises what our consciences already know, if we were only honest with ourselves: that when God says 'Love your neighbour' He means a love which willingly engages in positive acts of care and extravagant gestures of self-sacrifice, irrespective of the race, colour or creed of the one in need. A love which refuses to ask, as this lawyer did, 'Who?' but insists only on asking, 'How?' It is not interested in the possibility of evasion, only in finding opportunity for expression. It is a love not content to be merely applauded theoretically, but demanding to be demonstrated in practice. 'Go and do likewise,' He says.

I'm sure you don't need me to tell you how this world of ours would be turned upside down by such a love. It would work a social transformation far more radical than any economic revolution, whether from the left or from the right. Consider the 'charity at home' philosophy for instance. Take your newspaper and spend a few moments identifying how many of the intractable conflicts, problems and hurts that disturb our world are caused by people asking–just as the lawyer does–'Who is my neighbour?' We refuse to love with this universal willingness. We are constantly arguing that charity begins at home. We consistently adopt a clannishness that discriminates between 'them' and 'us'. Jew and Arab in Palestine, Catholic and Protestant in Northern Ireland, Serb and Croat in Yugoslavia, resurgent nationalism in the Soviet Union, endemic tribalism in black Africa, class prejudice and race prejudice here in Britain–the list goes on and on and on. It doesn't matter in which corner of the world you live, you find neighbour-love perverted by chauvinism and sectarianism into something which isn't love at all but just an enlightened form of self-interest. We must not be so blind as to think it isn't in our community or, indeed, in our church.

Or consider the 'I don't do anybody any harm' attitude. Hasn't it struck you how much appalling neglect of social responsibility in our modern world is justified by that phrase, 'I don't do anybody any harm'? Back in 1964, a classic example of this was acted out on the streets of New York. A young woman in her late twenties was attacked on her way home by an assailant who stabbed her repeatedly and took over half an hour to murder her. She screamed repeatedly for help, and at least 38 people peering through their apartment windows witnessed the crime. Not one even bothered to telephone the police. When they were asked later why they had done nothing, the answer was unanimous: 'We just didn't want to get involved.' An isolated incident? I'm afraid it isn't. Here's a clip from last Thursday's *Daily Mail*. 'Motorists in New York slowed down to watch as a man raped a three-year-old girl in broad daylight next to a busy road, but no one stopped to help her.'

Here is the sick world we live in. Jesus' parable is real life today. But in our city centres at night, there are not many Good Samaritans around to give the story a happy ending. Our Western society has become so preoccupied with its individualistic and materialistic priorities that nobody wants to get involved in anybody else's problem. We don't do anybody any harm. That's how we comfort ourselves, isn't it? The victims of crime, the victims of war, the victims of exploitation, the victims of oppression – what business are they of mine? These human tragedies that scar the world aren't *my* responsibility. So, just like the priest and the Levite, we pass by on the other side, comforting ourselves all the time with the excuse, 'We don't do anybody any harm.'

'Whatever you did not do for one of the least of these, you did not do for me' (Matt. 25:45) – we have it then from the mouth of Christ himself that sins of omission are so heinous, so culpable in God's sight, that they can damn us. For love is the fulfilment of the law. Confronted by the spectacle of human need, love can never stand idly by and do nothing.

I said yesterday that it was possible for social concern to so dominate the Christian agenda that we lose sight of the priority of evangelism. I don't step back from those words. The seed of the kingdom is the word. But let me say this morning that any Christian church that fails to demonstrate real social concern in a world like ours, no matter how zealous it may be in its evangelistic programme, will face the judgement of Christ. I believe that passionately. For the seed of the kingdom is the word, and that very word demands social concern. Social concern is part of the fruit of obedience which is the evidence of our fertility as soil. John Stott is surely right, then, when he insists that we may not pursue Christ's great commission, 'Go into all the world and preach the gospel,' to the neglect of His great commandment. 'This is My commandment,' He says: 'Love.'

There was a time, of course, when the Christian church in this country was, indeed, renowned for its practical obedience to that injunction of the Master. Even unsympathetic critics have to admit that in nineteenth-century England it was the evangelical believers who toiled indefatigably in the slums for the relief of the poor and the marginalised in society. Would that today, that was our media image! I fear it is not. The virus of individualistic self-indulgence which infects our Western society generally is very little resisted by evangelicalism today. Like the priest and the Levite, we are far more interested in the buzz we get from public worship than from the social responsibility which love demands.

The story of the Good Samaritan is as compelling, it seems to me, in its relevance to our twentieth-century world and to our twentieth-century church as when Jesus told it 2,000 years ago. I remember doing a Bible study with a small group of students, one of them from Latin America, many years ago, on this very parable or the Good Samaritan. His comment was, 'If only the church had told us this story and demonstrated to us this Jesus, many of my friends would have never have become Marxists.' For this is, without doubt, one of the most potent recipes for social change the world has ever heard: 'Go and do likewise.'

And yet the astonishing irony is this: *that wasn't why Jesus told the story.* Jesus did not tell this parable because He believed it could change the world. Indeed, if He did tell it for that purpose He must be feeling thoroughly disappointed now 2,000 years on, for it manifestly hasn't.

Now Jesus is no utopian socialist. Recall again the question with which this whole incident began, for that is the key to it. 'Teacher, what must I do to inherit eternal life?' Here, remember, is a man under the monumental delusion that he can earn his ticket to heaven by good works. And the ultimate purpose of this story is to show that man that he could not. The only reason this scholar could deceive himself into thinking that he could earn his ticket to heaven that way was because he interpreted God's law of love in such a reductionist manner. Once the full extent of his moral obligation is made plain to him, once he examines his life without the fig-leaf of excuses and evasions to hide his failures behind, he quickly discovers that he is not the great moral expert he thought he was. He knows the theory all right, but the practice just isn't there.

We could not be further from the truth, then, when we suggest that Jesus was confirming this man in his judaistic legalism when He says, 'Do this and you will live.' On the contrary, the whole point of His conversation is to strike a hammer-blow at that moral complacency of his. How do you think this man went away? What was the expression on his face?

That's the real reason this story stands in Luke's Gospel. We misunderstand it completely if we think it is only interested in teaching us our moral duty. It is intended, rather, to expose to us our moral bankruptcy. The Good Samaritan is Jesus' demolition job on the self-righteousness of those who dare to justify themselves. 'Face up to the performance gap in your life,' the parable says. 'You know God's standards of love, but you don't keep them. Go away and try to keep them if you're so sure you can. But once you stop rationalising your way out of the full force of God's command, once you stop emasculating the demands of love with comforting cliches like "Charity begins at home", and "I never do anybody any harm", once you start comparing your loving with the extravagant generosity of that Good Samaritan of Mine—then you will realise what a moral failure you really are. You will not come to Me then asking pompous, self-inflated questions like "What must I do to inherit eternal life?" '

No. Rather, like a man in the next story we shall be studying, you will be found with your head bowed, beating your breast, saying 'God be merciful to me, a sinner.' May I ask of you: have you got to that point of self-despair yet? Have you experienced such conviction of sin? For it is a frighteningly rare experience in our churches today. Do you come to Jesus this morning for a debate—or for a rescue?

Once we do get to the point where we know we need a rescue, we shall discover there is a further dimension yet to this remarkable story of the Good Samaritan; perhaps the most precious dimension of all.

I said yesterday that the parables were often abused during the Middle Ages, as a result of the allegorical interpretation of medieval scholars. This story of the Good Samaritan suffered more than most in that regard. The great Augustine, for instance, tells us that the wounded man represents Adam; that Jerusalem from which he journeys represents the state of innocence from which Adam fell. The thieves who beat him up are the devil who deprived Adam of eternal life, the priest and the Levite are Old Testament religion which passed by and cannot help him, and the Good Samaritan, of course, is Christ, who comes to his rescue. The inn to which he takes him is the church, the two coins which are given for his care are the sacraments of baptism and the mass, and the innkeeper, self-evidently, is the pope!

Well, suffice it to say there is no evidence at all that Jesus intended His story to be understood in such a fashion. And yet, those medieval scholars were not without their spiritual insight, were they? For even if the Good Samaritan was not intended to be an allegorical representation of the mission of Christ, it is true to say that Christ is the perfect fulfilment of the command to love, which the Good Samaritan illustrates.

There is a man who travelled that Jericho road, but in the opposite direction. Toward Jerusalem, not away from it, and with a cross on His back. And from that cross the Story-teller this morning repeats to us that old commandment of love. Only, because He is saying it, it has somehow now also become a new commandment. 'Love one another,' He says, 'as I have loved you.' Moses could never have added that second clause, could he? Nor could the lawyer. But Jesus can. For He has turned the Good Samaritan from fiction into fact. Here is a love that breaks down the artificial barriers of race and tribe and class. Here is a love that is not satisfied with mere passive goodwill but insists upon active, extravagant sacrificial service. 'Love one another,' He says, 'as I have loved you. You can love that way, now; because, unlike Moses, I have not only brought you the command to love – I have brought you the power to love. My Spirit poured out from heaven will shed abroad the love of God in your hearts. Go and do likewise.'

To those who, like this lawyer, think they can earn their ticket to heaven by good deeds, Jesus' words are a challenge to face up to their true moral inadequacy. You don't love like this; you can't love like this. You don't *want* to love like this. Stop fooling yourself!

But to those who have learnt that lesson, who have come to Christ in repentance and faith, confessing their failure and sin, the challenge of these final words comes afresh a second time and with even more force. 'Go and do likewise,' He says. 'Prove the quality of a Spirit-filled life which I have given you. All men will know you are My disciples if you love one another as I have loved you.'

This is an immensely practical story, and it demands that we do not rest satisfied with platitudinous responses to God in the wake of it. So I want us to think of one or two very practical, specific things in our lives that we must do if we are to even start to love our neighbour as the Good Samaritan suggests we should. Maybe in the family context – somebody who's becoming neglected in the family circle to whom we need to give much more attention? Maybe in the church context – a tense relationship we need to heal? Maybe in our work context; in the neighbourhood we live in; in the extended family of relatives and in-laws?

Wherever it is, let's face up to the challenge of love and identify some very practical, specific things that we must do if we are to 'go and do likewise.'

3. The Paradox of Pardon
(Luke 18:9–14)

Jack and Joe went to church one evening. Jack knew his way around. Well, he'd been brought up in the place, hadn't he? Sunday School from the age of three, and all that. He knew his parents would be there too in one of the other pews watching him proudly. He wanted to make sure they saw him. So he walked right up to the front and sat in the first row. He bowed his head and shut his eyes for a few moments – he'd seen Dad do that, he knew it looked holy.

Jack, you see, took his religion very seriously. He carried a big Bible and knew all the latest choruses. He liked the image of being a highly principled young man, too. Unlike many of his peers he never consumed alcohol or cigarettes. He was also extremely self-righteous about sex. No messing around behind the school bike sheds for him. He and his girlfriend had intellectual conversations about vegetarianism and the nuclear issue. Instead of going to discos they went to prayer meetings at the Youth Leader's house.

As Jack reflected on his life in those few moments before the service began, he glowed with inward satisfaction. How reassuring it was to know that you were a good Christian! Nothing to confess, nothing to feel ashamed about, nothing—

Good grief, it couldn't be! Out of the corner of his eye he caught sight of a familiar figure who had just entered the church behind him. 'It's Joe,' he thought incredulously.

'What on earth is he doing here? He's no right to come to church, the old hypocrite.' But if he had been able to read Joe's mind he would have realised that precisely the same thoughts were going through his head too.

What right did he have to be in church? He hadn't been in church for years, in fact he felt thoroughly uncomfortable in the place. He kept looking around nervously as if he expected somebody in authority to appear at any moment and tell him he had no business to be there. He was unsure where to sit, or if there was some special ritual he should observe before committing himself to stay. Didn't Christians cross themselves before they sat down in church? Or was that Moslems—he really couldn't remember. In the end he slid cautiously into the very back row. 'Oh no,' he wailed, 'that's Jack in the front and he's seen me. I'll never live this down in the neighbourhood now.' He crumpled up, his legs tucked under the pew, his head sagging down between his knees, trying to hide.

As you may have guessed, Joe was not the religious sort. In fact he had a reputation as a bit of a lad. If there was trouble with the police on the estate, you could bet your last dollar he'd be involved. Nicotine stained his fingers and there was a distinct smell of beer on his breath, in fact he'd been in the pub down the road only fifteen minutes before.

Why on earth had he come to church? Was it because of the row he'd had that morning at home, thrown out on his ear for stealing his mother's housekeeping again? Or was it because of the sense of humiliation he was feeling as a result of Julie slapping him around the face last night and telling him in unambiguous four-letter words to get out of her life—just because she discovered he was also sleeping with Karen? Yes, it was both of those things and neither of them. Somehow as he tried unsuccessfully to drown his sorrows in that pint he'd just been overcome with a sense of how dirty he was, and what a mess he'd made of things. Suddenly, sitting in that back pew, guilt and shame brought tears to his eyes, a blush to his cheek and a lump to his throat. 'Oh, God' he sighed quietly, into clenched fists. 'Oh God.'

I tell you, it was Joe who went home saved that night, not

Jack. 'For everyone who exalts himself will be humbled, and he who humbles himself will be exalted' (18:14).

We said in our first study that one of the great problems in reading the parables today is the difficulty of recovering the shock factor that they undoubtedly possessed for Jesus' original hearers. Too often, familiarity with these stories has disarmed them of their punch for us.

Take the story of the Good Samaritan which we studied yesterday. The very word 'Samaritan' has become proverbial for goodness. So when Jesus tells that it was a Samaritan who stopped to help the injured man we're not surprised, still less outraged. There's no scandalised intake of breath at the mere mention of the word, as there certainly would have been when the parable was first told. The hammer-blows the parable delivered to the prejudices of Jesus' original audience are reduced, for us, to the caress of a reassuring feather. We know all about Good Samaritans.

Even more is that true of the parable to which we turn this morning. I have retold it in modern dress in an attempt to help us feel more powerfully the contradiction of conventional expectation that it represents.

Think about it for a moment. Two men went up to the temple to pray. A self-evidently laudable ambition, you would have thought. Both came to pray and both went home believing sincerely they had prayed. Yet the extraordinary lesson of this parable is that while one of them truly did have dealings with God in his devotions that day, the other–in spite of his avowed good intentions–was conducting a soliloquy all the time he was in the temple.

The text which my version renders 'prayed about himself' (verse 11), could I suspect be more accurately translated 'Prayed *to* himself'. It was a soliloquy. That alone should be sufficient to worry us, shouldn't it? For we have clearly come to Keswick with the same intention as these two men, to meet with God. Yet Jesus says it is possible to come to the house of prayer thinking that you want to meet with God, to leave the house of prayer thinking you have done so, and all the time be self-deceived. What a disturbing challenge to the reality of our own spiritual experience that must be!

But the paradox is even sharper than that. And it's here

that the modern reader so easily forfeits the scandalous element in the story. For Jesus tells us that the man whose prayer was heard was a tax man. For us, that occasions no surprise. In our society representatives of the Inland Revenue generally speaking are pillars of the establishment; we make occasional sarcastic jokes about them but none of us would question their respectability.

Not so this tax man. In Jesus' day a tax man was a crook, a treacherous, despicable collaborator with the Roman enemy, who made himself rich by exploiting his fellow countrymen. Think of some provincial mayor lining his fat pockets in occupied France during the days of the Occupation by licking the boots of the Nazis, and you get the feel of how Jews felt about tax men in the first century. They didn't make sarcastic jokes about tax men, they lynched them. They spat on them when they passed and cursed the ground they walked on. Yet God heard the *tax man's* prayer–the very person they would never have listened to, let alone helped, in a thousand years.

On the other hand the man who went home unheard, Jesus tells us, was a pharisee. Once again, as modern readers we so easily miss the outrage of such a suggestion. For if we know from childhood that Samaritans are proverbially good, then even more do we know from childhood that pharisees are proverbially bad. As soon as Jesus identifies this man as a pharisee we conclude that he's going to be the villain of the piece. All kinds of negative and damning associations flow into our minds at the mere mention of the word pharisee.

Once again, such would not have been the reaction of Jesus' original hearers. For the pharisee was the churchman, the Bible student: fundamentalist in his view of scripture, scrupulous in his observance of God's law–a patriot, a philanthropist, a model of holiness, an enthusiastic supporter of Mary Whitehouse, 'Keep Sunday Special', the Moral Majority.

If this man was alive today, you know where he would be? He'd be here at Keswick. You know what we would call him? We would call him an evangelical Christian. In fact, if this pharisee was with us today there is every possibility he would be up here on the platform. That's what pharisees were. They were the first century equivalent of Keswick Convention speakers!

Now do you see the paradox, the shock? Jesus said it's a Keswick Convention speaker whose prayer God ignored. What an extraordinary tale! Can Jesus be serious? Could it be that even some of us–yes, even the most morally respectable, biblically learned, doctrinally sound, eminently honoured among us–will return home at the end of this week congratulating ourselves that once again we have received a Keswick blessing–while the truth is that all the time we've been here we've been doing nothing more spiritually beneficial than talking to ourselves?

This is one parable the shock factor of which we just can't afford to miss. Jesus has got something vital to teach us here about the whole nature of religion, of prayer, of guilt, of righteousness; and we dare not allow our twentieth-century images of tax men and pharisees to blunt the force of his warnings.

So try hard with me this morning to get under the surface of this parable into the shoes of Jesus' original hearers, and benefit from it, as we of all people in Keswick today need to benefit from it.

Two kinds of prayer

What was so wrong with the pharisee's prayer and right about the tax man's prayer, that God's assessment of them should be so radically different from our expectations? I don't think it's difficult to spot. Notice how the pharisee begins. 'Lord' he says 'I thank you that I am not like other men.'

Can you imagine going to your doctor and saying 'I want you to know that I am in superb health: my lungs are functioning perfectly, my muscle-tone is ideal, my digestion couldn't be better, my circulation is A1, I have no infections, no ailments, no diseases. In short, Doctor, unlike the rest of the miserable specimens I observe in your waiting room, there's absolutely nothing wrong with me at all.'

What could a doctor do for such a man? He would leave the surgery unchanged, unbenefited in any way. There's little point in visiting at all, except to parade as a kind of one-man medical beauty show. He could receive nothing, because he asked for nothing. And why does he ask for nothing? Because he feels no need.

Had he allowed the doctor to examine him his confidence may have been rather diminished. 'Your blood pressure's a bit high' the doctor might have said. 'And we must do some tests on that mysterious lump, and I would let the dentist have a look at that tooth if I were you. And did you know you were diabetic?' But such is his complacency, he never invites such an examination. The absence of any felt-need renders his attendance at the doctor's clinic totally redundant.

And this is exactly the point Jesus makes in another saying: 'It is not the healthy who need a doctor, but the sick' (Matt. 9:12). This pharisee is a perfect example of that observation. He came into the temple to congratulate himself on his spiritual and moral health. Augustine wisely comments on him, 'Thou hast said thou hast all, thou hast asked for nothing – in what respect then hast thou come to pray?' He hadn't come to pray at all, but to prate. It was all exhibitionist boasting and nothing more.

And haven't we all heard it ourselves? At evangelical prayer meetings. 'Look at what an outstanding Christian I am!' says the Prayer. 'Observe all the Bible verses I'm able to quote. Just look at all the spiritual passion I'm able to display, all the worldliness I'm able to condemn.' Of how many public prayers have you quietly said to yourself: 'That wasn't a prayer, that was a sermon. And I know exactly who it was preached against.'?

The tax man knew for whose benefit the pharisee's sermon was being preached. He overheard him, of course – how could he help it? 'God, I thank you' said the pharisee at the top of his voice, 'that I'm not like other men, rogues, swindlers, traitors, or like that tax man over there.' Every word was a deliberate dig at him. But then he was used to such abuse. He didn't resent it, why should he? He knew he deserved it, he was under no illusions about his moral and spiritual condition, he was painfully aware of the disease of his soul. There was a mark of judgement set against his destiny, he knew.

And for this reason we hear no self-congratulatory expressions of mock gratitude from his lips. He feels his need. As he beats his breast with the sense of it – a gesture no Jew made except in times of profound emotional distress—his need bursts out of him in three staccato gasps of inner torture. 'God be merciful to me–*the* sinner'. That's what he says literally. '*The* sinner'–for at that moment he felt like the only sinner in the universe. Yet, says Jesus, that's the kind of prayer God hears. That sort of worshipper goes home a different person, whereas the proud and complacent, for all their eloquent supplications, leave the house of God in exactly the same unacceptable state in which they arrived. One recalls Mary's words: 'He has filled the hungry with good things but has sent the rich away empty' (Luke 1:53).

I want to suggest to you: this question of personal felt need may very well be the crunch issue for many here. How hungry are we for God? How desperate are we for His grace? It is that, perhaps more than anything else, which will determine whether or not we have real dealings with Him at this Convention.

Much has been said in recent years about the renewal of worship in the church; in fact it made the headlines when the Archbishop of Canterbury was enthroned. But it does seem to me that much of that controversy is concerned with things of interest to the pharisee but not to the tax man. It's concerned with matters of external form. What type of music–traditional hymns or modern choruses? What sort of atmosphere–quiet and meditative or loud and excited? What kind of congregational participation–passive and restrained or active and exuberant? What degree of predictability – fixed prayer-book liturgy or extemporary charismatic spontaneity? These are the issues.

Frankly, while that sort of debate may well signal major changes in worship style, I'm not at all convinced that it has anything to do with renewal of worship in the spiritual sense at all.

Charles M. Schulz, the 'Peanuts' cartoonist, suggested thirty years ago that most people attending church on Sunday do so with the same feelings as they attend the theatre; simply to enjoy what's going on. And he was absolutely right, in my view. The only thing he didn't take note of is that there are different kinds of entertainment, and how you express your enjoyment depends on the nature of the event. Schulz is

quite right that some people come to church to sit passively
listening as if at the theatre. But there are others who come
with the same attitude with which they would attend a football match. And there are others who come with the same
attitude with which they would attend a disco. With whatever
attitude they come however, they all come to enjoy what's
going on. The worship style in which the church engages is no
ground at all on which to judge the spirituality of those who
are participating. Indeed, those of us who have travelled
know that worship style is largely culturally determined. You
go to a black Baptist church in the southern states of the USA
and then to a Free Presbyterian in the Scottish highlands and
compare the difference! But that difference has nothing
whatever to do with the spiritual authenticity of the worshippers. It's a cultural difference.

What determines whether we have real dealings with God
when we go into His house to pray is not the music or the
atmosphere, nor even the degree of our physical participation in it. To think of worship in such terms is to think like
a Judaistic pharisee and not like a Christian at all. It is the
hallmark of new covenant religion that it is indifferent to
cultural forms. 'Neither on this mountain nor in Jerusalem,'
Jesus told the woman of Samaria, 'will people worship. A
time is coming and has now come when true worshippers will
worship the Father in spirit and truth, for they are the kind of
worshippers the Father seeks.'

You want to know why that tax man was heard? It was
because he had a heart for God. He felt the need for God.
Worship for him was a matter of spirit and truth. That's why
he went to church—not to be entertained, nor, like the pharisee, to entertain others. He went there like a sick man goes
to a doctor, because he felt a profound personal moral desperation. God always hears the prayers of people like that,
whoever they are: crooks, rogues, adulterers—why, He even
heard the eleventh-hour appeal of a thief on the cross. But
He ignores, He snubs those who come to His house as if they
were attending a circus, simply to enjoy what's going on.
After all, it's not as though they come to meet Him, is it!

You and I will never have real dealings with God, we will
never truly pray, until we get beyond religious entertainment,

until we stop coming to churches or even Keswick Conventions simply to enjoy what's going on; until we reach this point of felt need which the tax man had reached. Then we will pray and get answers.

Two kinds of guilt

Jesus highlights for us in this paradoxical little story two kinds of guilt. It becomes more ironic, you know, the more you think about it: there was the tax man *feeling* guilty, yet Jesus says he went home acquitted; and yet there's the pharisee *feeling* innocent, and Jesus implies he went home condemned. That pin-points for us a very important distinction, between guilt as an emotional experience and guilt as an objective fact. And this little story points out that the presence or absence of the former doesn't necessarily imply the presence or absence of the latter.

We all know that there is such a thing as irrational guilt, guilt which feels out of proportion to any wrong we've actually committed. Psychiatrists have to deal with that kind of anxiety all the time. But what many people forget today is that it is equally possible to feel no guilt at all when in fact we should feel guilty. A complacent conscience may be psychologically innocuous. It may reduce our stress levels. I'm sure the pharisee was far more relaxed and at ease with himself than this tax man was. And yet in ultimate spiritual terms, such a complacent conscience is dreadfully perilous.

There is such a thing as real guilt. Guilt isn't just a feeling, it is a fact. Unfortunately the feeling and the fact don't always run together. In our increasingly psychologically aware generation we must not allow that objective reality of guilt to become obscured. Some years ago I had a discussion with some GCSE English students who were studying Shakespeare's *Macbeth*. We were discussing the scene where Lady Macbeth, after the murder, is wracked with anxiety about the image of blood which she sees indelibly clinging to her hands.

What struck me was that their reaction was almost unanimous: not 'Here is a vicious criminal dreadfully convicted of her sin, who badly needs to find a sense of forgiveness', but 'Here is a pathetic nutcase, seriously mentally disturbed, badly in need of a psychiatrist'.

Guilt has ceased to be an acceptable part of normal human experience in the twentieth century. It has become pathological. It's a symptom of emotional illness or mental abnormality now, rather than an appropriate moral response to personal sin. No longer do we send the guilt-stricken individual to the priest for absolution as we once did; we send them to the psychiatrist for treatment. And increasingly people think of the church itself as nothing more than an alternative form of such treatment. They go to church in order to feel better about themselves, in order to feel that they are OK people.

And that, I suggest to you, was precisely the function of the pharisee's piety. His religion was just a form of psychotherapy by which he got rid of his guilt feelings. Notice the three very obvious techniques he uses.

First, _he majors on negative obedience_. I commented on this in relation to the behaviour of the priest and the Levite in the story of the Good Samaritan. Here it is again. Our pharisee comforts himself with all the sins he has _not_ committed, like robbery or adultery. This is always good for the peace of our conscience, because of course such negative obedience forms a convenient smoke-screen behind which we may conceal the many sins we _have_ committed.

It's the kind of attitude which as we said in our second study is responsible for a great deal of evasion of social responsibility today. It enables people to see a murder committed on a city street and do nothing about it, because they aren't personally holding the knife.

It's also the reason, incidentally, that religion has such a kill-joy image in many people's minds. All those 'Thou-shalt-nots'. Many think of God as a prohibitive spoil-sport who wants to stop us doing all the things we want to do. Joy Davidman tells a lovely story of a missionary trying to convert an African chief. On being told that a long list of sins were indeed prohibited by Christian morality, he remarked that he was much too old to commit any of them anyway. 'So to be old and a Christian, they are the same thing!'

For many, that is exactly what being a Christian is: being old, being past it, giving oneself to God when the devil wants nothing more to do with us. They picture Christianity as something sapless and joyless, the enemy of all delights. And they think that way because so many religious people are trying to escape guilt by defining obedience in purely negative terms.

Second, *he majors on legalistic obedience*. He lists all the unnecessary 'good works of supererogation'–which he doesn't really have to do at all. Like fasting twice a week, when Moses said once a year was quite enough; like giving a tithe of absolutely everything he had, even the herbs in the kitchen which he used for flavouring his food, when Moses said a tithe of one's income was adequate.

Once again, legalism of this kind is a classic method of guilt-avoidance. By accumulating a record of this kind of superfluous piety you can deceive yourself into thinking that you're compensating for any real sins that you may have committed. It's quite illogical, of course, for if you think about it, you'll realise you can never make up for anything by subsequent penances of this sort. It's like going to the judge and saying 'Yes, I did drive at 100 mph down Helvellyn Street yesterday. But unlike some people I never park on a double yellow line. Surely you can take that into consideration.'

Yet there are thousands of religious people whose minds work essentially in that fallacious fashion. They are often obsessive personalities, preoccupied with the trivial details of their lives in a desperate attempt to camouflage, and compensate for, the formidable monster of moral corruption that they know secretly lurks within. As Jesus said, they spend their time straining gnats out of their soup and then go and swallow a camel. Some men take great pride in the fact that they don't smoke or drink, others are perfectionists in their hobbies, or workaholics in their careers. Some women are fanatically houseproud. They purge their conscience by liberal use of Dettol in the bathroom. And of course there are those endless numbers of religious people who salve their consciences by attending church, giving money to charity, saying prayers, etc. etc. There's a certain kind of compulsive personality that enjoys ritual, discipline, self-denial and that sort of thing. Ascetic, puritanical lifestyle is a form of self-indulgence for them.

And that's what the pharisees were like. All such

behaviour is driven by the desire to avoid guilt. By concentrating on the observance of petty rules and regulations which we set ourselves, rules which, though irksome, we know we can fully keep if we really try, our attention is diverted from God's rules, with regard to which our obedience can never be satisfactory and which therefore provide us with an inexhaustible source of potential moral anxiety.

Third, he *majors on comparative obedience*. 'I am not' he says, 'like other men, that tax man for instance.' This strategy of self-justification never fails, for there are always people more guilty than ourselves. That is why we read the gutter press; to feed our own smug self-satisfaction. 'Tut, tut!' we say under our self-righteous breath as we read the salacious headlines. 'Who could imagine somebody doing such a thing?'–the implication being 'I never would.'

Our moral censure of others is just a device to distract attention from our own guilt. We think that by adopting a tone of shocked indignation over the sins of others, our own sin will go unnoticed. Like Jesus says, we point out the speck in other people's eyes in order to distract attention from the great plank in our own. Like Paul says in Romans 2, we try to escape judgement by making ourselves into judges. By this type of comparative obedience many of us will probably succeed today in avoiding the chastening effect of this very parable upon our lives.

Do you know the story of the Sunday School teacher who told this story to his class? Afterwards he drew what he thought was the obvious moral lesson. 'Now, children,' he said, 'Let's thank God we're not like that proud pharisee.' The trouble is it's all too easy for conservative Bible-believing Christians like us to slip into the pharisee's shoes without even realising we're doing it, in the very act of trying to distance ourselves from him.

By these three classic techniques our pharisee succeeds in feeling good about himself. By these means he coped with his guilt feelings very well. So very well that they had been completely repressed. No flutter of moral anxiety disturbed this man's conscience at all. And yet Jesus insists: for all the effectiveness of his self-administered psychotherapy his real guilt remained. It had not been diminished one jot. He *felt* all right, but his *feelings* did not correspond to the state of his soul. He might have been more emotionally stable as a result of his religious exercises, but he was nearer hell.

Am I not right, then, to be concerned that there may be many in our churches suffering from the very same delusion? Or that I myself may be falling into this very same trap–by using this very parable to critique the religion of others when I should rather be examining myself? How do I deal with my guilt? That's the issue. Am I content simply to ease the pangs of conscience by persuading myself 'I'm OK, thank you very much'–or do I, like that tax man, yearn for some much more radical solution than that, to the pollution of my soul?

I remember very well this issue of handling guilt was brought home to me some years ago with peculiar force. I had to counsel a young woman university student, who had just had an abortion to avoid the inconvenience of a pregnancy that would have interrupted her degree course. To her surprise she found herself overwhelmed with guilt in the aftermath of the operation. So devastated was she by what she had done she had even attempted suicide, and that's why I'd been asked to see her. What do you say to a girl like that?

I'll tell you what a lot of her friends were saying. They were saying 'Don't be so silly. You're just suffering from a form of post-natal depression, it's your hormones. You've got nothing to be ashamed of. Snap out of it. What's the difference between an abortion and a spontaneous miscarriage?' Some of her colleagues were studying psychology, and had gladly analysed her guilt feelings in terms of Freud and Jung. She herself was a social scientist and was well aware of the argument that all moral convictions are just the result of human societal conditions. I've no doubt if she'd looked hard enough she could have found some remote tribe somewhere that regularly procure abortions without any conscience about it whatsoever. But she still felt guilty. And no amount of rationalising would take the feeling away.

She had discovered what her friends–employing the modern secular equivalents of pharisaical religion–had succeeded in hiding from themselves; that guilt is real. It's not just a mental state. She did not want to be sent to the psychiatrist to get her guilt neurosis erased. She didn't want to be reassured

with the smooth talk of some non-directive student counsellor. She didn't want to be de-programmed like one of
Pavlov's dogs. She wanted to be treated like a responsible
human being. What she wanted was not some therapy to
make her feel better but an answer to the guilt she had
incurred; a guilt which she was persuaded was not a psychological aberration, but an objective stain on her life. She
wanted forgiveness.

She'd reached the same point of personal desperation as
the tax man. He wouldn't rationalise his guilt away either. He
wouldn't persuade himself that he wasn't so bad after all, or
try to cloak his sin with legalistic observances or unfavourable
comparisons with others. No. He makes no feeble excuses,
pleads no mitigating circumstances, offers no compensatory
penances. He simply begs 'God be merciful to me, a sinner.'
And, says Jesus, that man went home not just feeling better
but with his moral status dramatically reversed in the eyes of
God.

Two kinds of righteousness

'I tell you that this man, rather than the other, went home
justified before God.'

'Justified' is a word not from the vocabulary of the psychiatrist but from the law courts. It does not describe how the
tax man *felt*. It describes how he stood legally before God's
bar of justice. It means quite literally that God had declared
him innocent. Just as a judge might acquit an accused person,
so God had passed a verdict of 'not guilty' on this conscience-
stricken man. And he would have us learn from this story
that the discovery of such justification is what true religion is
all about. It is the spiritual remedy by which we are liberated,
not just from guilt feelings but from the fact of guilt. It's not
just a method for easing our consciences. Justification is
about the cleansing of our lives. It's not just a psychological
analgesic. It is a moral purgative.

Martin Luther wrote, 'There are only two sorts of people
in the world: sinners who think themselves righteous, and the
righteous who think themselves sinners.' It's a bold generalisation, as Luther's so often are, and it needs qualification if

it's not to be misunderstood, but essentially he's right. And
the pharisee and tax man epitomise the point he's making.

Fundamentally the difference between these two was the
grounds upon which they sought acquittal in the eyes of God.
The pharisee was one of those who, Luke observes, 'were
confident of their own righteousness and looked down on
everybody else' (18:9). He could make it to heaven by his
own efforts. He would have nothing to be ashamed of before
God's tribunal. Why, he'd be able to boast about how hard
he had worked to get there.

How many tragic people there are in our churches every
Sunday who tread that path! I sometimes think this is going
to be the greatest irony of hell, that it will be full, not of
shame or even regret, but of self-righteous indignation. Many
of those there will be convinced that they don't deserve it.
'How dare God damn me' they'll be saying, 'after all I did for
Him?' Sometimes I shudder to imagine the shock that there
will be on that last day, as they present their self-manufactured ticket at the gate of heaven and hear it declared coun-
terfeit. 'I never knew you' He will say, 'depart from Me' (see
Matthew 7:22)

Why do they try it on? Jesus surely puts His finger on the
nub of the matter in that postscript: 'Everyone who exalts
himself will be humbled' he says, 'but he who humbles himself will be exalted.' It was conceit that lay at the root of the
pharisee's religion. He wanted to get to heaven with his
dignity unscathed. He wanted to go through those pearly
gates with his head held high. He wanted a righteousness he
could be proud of. But no such righteousness exists. For, as a
matter of unvarying policy on God's part, everyone who
exalts himself will be humbled.

This is the essential lesson of Jesus's only example. He
accepts the title 'Lord', but He takes the role of a servant. He
shares equality with God, but He hangs voluntarily on a
cross. No wonder the offended and perplexed people. In
those days humility was a vice, a despicable sign of weakness.
Yet Jesus insists that not only must we be humble, He reveals
in His incarnation and in His passion that the heart of God
Himself is humble.

No wonder this pharisee can't go to heaven then; he is

contemptuous of humanity. Whereas for the tax man it was his only hope of salvation: 'God have mercy on me the sinner.' Again, it's a weak translation, for that word 'mercy' is associated with the sacrificial ritual of the temple. It's not the normal word for 'mercy' at all. In fact if we were going to translate accurately in English we'd have to use an old-fashioned phrase like 'be propitiated towards me'.

This tax man's hope is not just in God's loving and compassionate nature. Remember where he is. His eyes are on that altar up there, where the temple priest at the hour of prayer has just offered sacrifice for the sins of the people. 'Please, God,' he says 'I see the blood stains there on the altar. Accept that sacrifice on my behalf, be propitiated towards me.' He's not just appealing to God's better nature when he says 'Be merciful to me.' He's laying claim to God's own remedy for the sinner's plight. And in doing so, of course, he highlights one more vital lesson that a morally complacent world too easily forgets: that there can be no real assurance of pardon without an act of atonement that satisfies God.

Some people think that forgiveness is easy for God. 'Of course God will forgive me' they say, 'it's His business.' Not so, not so at all. It's dreadfully hard for God to forgive sin. He's the moral governor of the universe. If He overlooks a sin it's as good as saying sin doesn't matter. The integrity of His own righteousness means that He must disassociate Himself from wickedness wherever He sees it. He can't lay Himself open to the charge of moral indifference or moral inconsistency. If He did, He wouldn't be God any longer. And that's why in Old Testament times there had to be a temple, there had to be an altar, there had to be a sacrifice.

That sacrifice was first of all the symbol of the seriousness of sin in God's eyes. We human beings are squeamish about blood. Well, God is squeamish about sin. He is repulsed by its stench and stain. That blood sacrifice on the altar was the symbol of his moral revulsion.

More than that, though: sacrifice was the symbol of the penalty of sin. For as blood speaks of death, so sin demands death. No less a price is adequate to express the horror and the indignation of a holy God. Forgiveness may be offered freely in the Bible, but never make the mistake of thinking it's cheap. The Bible knows nothing of cheap forgiveness. Our tax man knew that. 'Oh God' he said, 'be propitiated towards me, let my sin be atoned for. I don't minimise the seriousness of my crimes. I don't underestimate the penalty they deserve. I see the blood, I know the cost, so please God turn your anger from me, be satisfied that that sacrificial substitute has died on the altar in my place today. And so have mercy on me the sinner.'

It may seem strange to ask a congregation at a Keswick Convention this question, but I fear I must. Have you asked God's pardon, the tax man's way? Or do you seek a right-eousness like the pharisee's, built on your religious reputation and your moral achievements? Do you come here today to convince yourself you're okay, thank you God? To feel good about yourself? Is listening to these Bible readings a kind of protestant equivalent of flagellation, a penance you endure in order to convince yourself that you're really a good Christian?

Or are you like the tax man, longing for the righteousness that rests on God's merciful provision of an atoning sacrifice?

Extraordinary as it may sound, I find pastorally there are an enormous number of professing Christians today – and I mean evangelical Christians – who come to church regularly to pray and yet have never really made this most fundamental discovery. Deep down they know they are guilty but instead of resolving their guilt God's way, they bury it.

The symptoms of that buried guilt are so easy to spot. A lack of self-esteem, a low self-image, an inferiority complex. They go around complaining 'I'm no good at being a Christian. I don't feel excited about being a Christian, I've got no assurance of salvation, no joy in worship, no enthusiasm to witness, I'm a lame-duck Christian, that's what I am.' Countless people are burdened in this way. They say they're depressed, that they can't cope, that they always make a mess of things, that they're no use to anybody and it's pointless trying to improve themselves. What's wrong with these people? What's the source of this spiritual debility?

I don't want to over-simplify by generalisation. The pastoral problems involved may be very complex. But I am convinced that a considerable proportion of these folk are suffering from unresolved feelings of repressed guilt. Christians though they are or say they are, their attitudes are shaped by this guilt-denying world of ours. And as a result they have never been truly convicted of sin, never properly understood God's remedy for sin, and therefore have never really felt truly pardoned of sin. That's why they feel inadequate, that's why assurance eludes them. The one person you can never forgive is yourself. So long as this spectre of unacknowledged guilt deep within their psyche haunts them, they will continue to suffer the destructive consequences of sub-conscious self-hatred eating away inside them, destroying their motivation, their ambition, their assurance.

What's the answer? The answer is they must come and stand where the tax man stood. Justification by faith must cease to be a cerebral article of their creed and become instead an experimental truth in their hearts. They must stand where the tax man stood, with all the defensive masks removed, all the illusions of moral respectability shattered, all pretence of self-righteousness abandoned. They must look where the tax man looked, to a sacrifice; but to a far nobler and more costly sacrifice than ever was slain on a temple altar. They must look to a cross where the Son of God Himself shed His blood once and for all, to make atonement for the sin of the world. And they must pray as that tax man prayed, 'God have mercy on me, I ask for no cheap forgiveness, I do not underestimate the seriousness of my crime. I know the penalty of my sin is death, but please God be satisfied that a worthy substitute has paid the price in my place and so be merciful to me the sinner.'

And most of all, they need to hear that reassuring verdict of Jesus upon such a penitential prayer: 'I tell you this man went home justified.' He stood in the presence of God now not as a despised and condemned criminal, but as a beloved and accepted child. Justified by faith he could now have peace with God. Not the peace of the pharisee, that self-manufactured psychological fiction which would one day be stripped from him to his horror in final judgement. No, a peace with God based on God's own irreversible, incontestable declaration of pardon, through Jesus's blood.

Our Convention's nearly at an end. Will we go home any different from the way we came, I wonder? It will depend on what kind of prayer we prayed. Have we just engaged in pious theatricals, or have we come here because we feel a great need for God? It will depend on how we dealt with our guilt. Are we content merely with a little religious therapy that enables us to feel good about ourselves, or do we long for a radical cleansing of the real guilt that lies on our souls? It will depend on what sort of righteousness we seek. A righteousness of our own that comes through our own moral efforts, or a righteousness from God that depends on faith?

I don't often quote from the great theologian Karl Barth and I'm certainly not recommending his writings to you, but he does express this very eloquently.

> We dislike hearing that we are saved by grace alone. We don't really appreciate that God does not owe us anything, that we are bound to live from His goodness alone, that we are left with nothing but the great humility of a child presented with many gifts. To put it bluntly, we do not like to believe.

But believe we must. Believe in the greatness of the merciful heart of God, believe in the sufficiency of Christ's atoning sacrifice. Believe most of all perhaps in the truth of that extraordinary promise, 'Everyone who exalts himself will be humbled, but he who humbles himself will be exalted.'

In the topsy-turvy world of heaven it is the poor who are rich, the humble who are great. In the paradoxical topography of the kingdom of God, the way up is down.

4. The Ultimate Insult:
(Luke 20:9–19)

G. K. Chesterton once commented that it's always easier to forgive an injury than an insult. I suspect he's right. Some people just seem to have a perpetual knack of opening their mouth and putting their foot in it. Everywhere they go they quite unintentionally make offensive and tactless remarks. But usually it's not too difficult to laugh off such clumsy insensitivity.

On the other hand, some insults are deliberate, premeditated and calculated to hurt, and they can deliver devastating emotional wounds–especially if those who deliver them are people close to us. I remember some years ago being shown a letter written by a daughter to her mother. It was the most concentrated verbal vitriol I have ever seen, and it broke that poor mother's heart. If her daughter had publicly spat in her face she could not have felt more profoundly humiliated.

'Sticks and stones may break my bones, but words can never hurt me.' That was the standard playground retort for such oral malice when I was at school. But the bluff is as poor as the rhyme, for names do hurt. Words have a capacity to draw tears and prey upon our minds, to sting our feelings in a way that no physical blow ever could.

Chesterton then is surely right when he says it's often easier to forgive an injury than an insult. Perhaps a memory of some such slap in the face is being kindled even as I speak. If so, you'll be able to empathise profoundly with this final

Bible reading today; for in Luke 20 Jesus is telling us the story of what I reckon can justly be called the most shameless, the most cruel insult ever administered in the history of the world. I've called it 'the ultimate insult'. No other insult has demonstrated more brazen impertinence, left such permanent scars or been so totally undeserved. For this insult was delivered not against a human being but against the loving heart of God Himself.

And Jesus tells us about it in the last of His parables which Luke records and which I think may well have been the last parable that Jesus ever told.

Some have argued that 'parable' is a misnomer for this story, for it comes closer to being a truer allegory than any of the other stories that we've studied this week. It's also considerably less cryptic. You don't have to struggle to interpret this one. Perhaps it is because Jesus is now only a matter of days from the end of His life that He feels that He can speak with more transparency than He's done before. So obvious is the meaning of this story that even unsympathetic listeners are in no doubt about what Jesus is getting at.

We are going to examine it in three stages this morning. First I want to ask: how did Jesus understand the human condition? The story answers that, I think, as it sets the scene for the insult.

Then I want to ask: how did Jesus understand His own mission? The story shocks us with the news of the insult, as it answers that question for us.

And thirdly I want to ask: how did Jesus understand the future? For this story of Jesus ends with some very solemn consequences and warnings.

How Jesus understood the human condition

'A man planted a vineyard...' (20:9)
Look back to verse 1 of this chapter, and you'll discover that Jesus told this parable in the context of another inquisition being conducted against Him by the chief priests and the teachers of the law. His journey to Jerusalem, which Luke has been narrating since chapter 9 in his Gospel, is at last complete. He has now entered the city amid a triumphant procession of His followers. And no sooner has He arrived

than He causes a minor sensation by throwing merchants out of the temple. Not surprisingly, the Jewish establishment feel that some kind of official enquiry into this hot-head's dubious credentials is required. Hence their loaded question: 'Tell us by what authority you are doing these things... Who gave you this authority?' (20:2).

Jesus however demonstrates once again His consummate skill in parrying this kind of hostile interrogation. He asks a loaded question of His own, refusing to answer their's directly. 'You tell me,' He says: 'John's baptism—was it from heaven, or from men?' (20:4).

And while they are fumbling to find a diplomatic answer which will not in some way incriminate or embarrass them, He goes straight on to tell this story.

It's a story which, according to verse 19, His inquisitors were convinced was directed against them personally. I'm sure they weren't victim to any irrational paranoia in entertaining that suspicion. Anyone familiar with the Old Testament knew that the imagery of the vineyard which Jesus uses was not original. He had borrowed it. The prophet Isaiah, 800 years earlier, composed an allegorical song along very similar lines to Jesus' parable here. And the relationship between the two is unmistakable.

'My loved one had a vineyard on a fertile hillside... he looked for a crop of good grapes, but it yielded only bad fruit. Now you dwellers in Jerusalem and men of Judah, judge between me and my vineyard. What more could have been done for my vineyard than I have done for it? When I looked for good grapes, why did it yield only bad? Now I will tell you what I am going to do with my vineyard: I will take away its hedge, and it will be destroyed; I will break down its wall, and it will be trampled' (Isa. 5:1–5).

Isaiah, however, interprets his allegory:

'The vineyard of the Lord Almighty is the house of Israel, and the men of Judah are the garden of his delight. And he looked for justice, but saw bloodshed; for righteousness, but heard cries of distress' (Isa. 5:7).

Isaiah's song was far too famous, and the parallels with Jesus' parable far too obvious, for the implication to be lost on these Jewish Bible scholars. The vineyard of which Jesus' parable speaks was the same as Isaiah's. It was Israel, the people of God. The one who planted this vineyard had to be God Himself. The servants He had sent as emissaries were clearly the prophets of the Old Testament. And the wicked tenants to whom Jesus attributes the blame for the vineyard's unproductiveness: who are they? Well, one did not need to use much imagination to realise that they represent Israel's leaders, the very chief priests and teachers of the law that were trying to discredit Jesus at that moment. They were fully justified in thinking it was preached against them.

It wasn't the first time that Jesus had publicly denounced the hierarchy of His nation in this way. Back in Luke 11 there is a pungent attack, including one comment that you could almost regard as a commentary on this parable: 'Woe to you experts in the law, because you build tombs for the prophets, and it was your forefathers who killed them. So you testify that you approve of what your forefathers did; they killed the prophets, and you build their tombs. Because of this, God in His wisdom said, "I will send them prophets and apostles, some of whom they will kill and others they will persecute." ' (Luke 11:47–49)

It is that strange divine strategy of sending His servants to a rejecting people that Jesus is allegorising here in His story. The people of God refused to yield the fruit of righteousness which He requires of them. Instead they cruelly reject His servants the prophets whenever He sends them.

The danger for us of course is that in recognising that the immediate reference of this parable was to Israel and to its leaders, we may evade its applications for us. We may say to ourselves perhaps, just as we did with the parable of the pharisee and the tax man: 'Ah, those hypocritical high priests and scribes! We all know what wicked people they were. Thank God we are not among the wicked tenants He speaks about.' And once again, the shock and the rebuke of the parable is lost on us.

That would be a disastrous mistake. For this parable of Jesus is no more limited in its relevance to the Israel of the first century AD than the song of Isaiah, which Jesus is re-expounding, was limited to the Israel of the eighth century BC. No, this is a story of privilege abused, generosity despised, and responsibility shirked. And as such, I suggest, it speaks to the human condition generally. Luke certainly doesn't include it in his Gospel to foster anti-semitic prejudice among his gentile readers. He included it because it was relevant to them.

I suggest to you, Jesus is not just describing Israel when He speaks of this vineyard. He is describing for us any and every situation in this fallen and rebellious planet where divine blessing is answered by human contempt. As such His words are of relevance to the visible church, a church which possesses the revelation of the word of God in a way far beyond anything Israel ever knew, but which again and again grieves the heart of God with its apostasy.

These words are relevant to this land of Britain, a land which has experienced the influence of God in a way far beyond the majority of the nations, but which today is almost as secularised and pagan as some which have never heard the gospel.

It's relevant to some of us too as individuals. For we have been blessed personally through the ministry of the word of God, far beyond many of our neighbours, yet like that seed which was sown in thorny ground it has produced so little fruit of obedience in our lives. Indeed I don't think it's an over-statement to say that Jesus is describing for us here in this parable the tragic condition of the whole world. A world which was originally created by God, full of productive potential; like a farm prepared with everything needed for prosperity, planted and equipped, needing only to be worked. God put Adam in the garden to till it and keep it for Him, we are told in Genesis 2.

So what's gone wrong with our world? Why have things turned sour and all our hopes foundered? Why do those optimistic dreams of a better society prove again and again to be elusive fantasies, like mirages in the desert?

A hundred years ago, at the very end of the nineteenth century, humanist intellectuals spoke with Promethean confidence about the glorious future that awaited the human race in the twentieth century; freedom from illness, war, poverty. The human race guided by science and technology, they said, was on a route to a new golden age. They were sure of it.

Everybody believed it. But instead, of course, these last hundred years have seen military conflict on an unprecedented global scale. They have witnessed famines of unparalleled dimensions. And as for freedom from illness— the medical science which has conquered smallpox and tuberculosis finds itself in the 1990s helpless before the pandemic scourge of the AIDS virus.

Now in the 1990s, just as in the 1890s, there are those who, encouraged by the arrival not just of a new century but of a new millenium, speak once more in utopian terms about the dawn of a 'New Age'. Strange, isn't it, how that row of noughts on the end of the year 2000 is invested with almost mystical significance?

I wonder under what twenty-first century horrors that optimism is going to be buried in our children's lifetimes. It doesn't bear thinking about. The idyllic dream of the Garden of Eden keeps returning to haunt the human race, but it is nothing but a dream, a tantalising unrealisable dream of paradise lost. Why is it, Jesus, that we human beings are forever more insecure and violent, the further we advance? What's gone wrong in the vineyard, Jesus?

Is it that these tenant farmers have not yet evolved sufficiently from their animal origins to co-operate harmoniously in tending the vines? Is that the problem? Is it that their science is too primitive, do they need to update their productive efficiency with mechanisation and fertilisers? Is it the vicious socio-economic system to which they are victim, with its oppressive absentee landlords and exploited labourers, seething with class antagonism?

No. According to Jesus it's none of these things. The problem is simple, He says. These people were placed in the vineyard as tenants, but they want to be owners. ' "This is the heir," they said. "Let's kill him, and the inheritance will be ours." ' (20:14)

A tenant, of course, is accountable to somebody. He pays the rent. And Jesus is saying here the same is true of human beings. We are accountable too. We owe a debt of moral obedience to the God who gave us this beautiful world to live in. That's why the word 'ought' features so prominently in our vocabulary. Originally the word 'ought' was part of the verb 'to owe'. It is the word of moral duty, of moral debt. Intuitively all human beings recognise its authority over them. We can distinguish quite easily in our decision making between what we want to do, what's easiest to do or what others are forcing us to do – and what we ought to do.

And we instinctively feel that final constraint upon our choices has an unquestionable priority over all others. No matter how painful or inconvenient it may be, no matter how many people are trying to make me do the opposite, if something is what I *ought* to do then I *ought* to do it. I'm obliged by an imperative taking precedence over every other consideration. We all understand that word 'ought', for it is the word of our tenancy, the word of our obligation.

The question of course that has occupied the minds of philosophers for thousands of years is, where does this extraordinary sense of obligation come from? Increasingly, people want to relate it to social conditioning. 'Morality?' they say. 'Oh, that's just a social convention. We're taught in our infancy certain things, and we internalise them in the form of a conscience as we grow up.' But the trouble is that once you really believe that that's all morality is, it immediately loses its cogency and has no power over you. If right and wrong are just human inventions, then why shouldn't we disregard them if we want to?

Modern sociological analysis of the word 'ought' doesn't so much explain our sense of moral obligation, as explain it away. Increasingly in our Western world we are experiencing the anarchy and the permissiveness that irresistibly results from that sort of corrosive scepticism. For the distinctive thing about the word 'ought' is that it has to come from outside us, from some higher authority. And the problem with the humanistic philosophy that has dominated our culture for the last two centuries is that it has no access to such a higher authority. Its followers want a moral law but without a moral law-giver. They want personal values without a personal God. And you can't have them.

Responsibility by definition involves two parties. You have to be able to answer the question 'Responsibility to whom?' Humanism can't answer that. That's why it's been such a disastrous interlude in our intellectual history.

But Jesus can answer the question. He understands where the word 'ought' comes from. It's the owner of the vineyard, He says. Our moral nature is just a reflection of the fact that we were put on this earth as tenants, not as owners. We owe something to our Creator. There is an inescapable 'ought' in the very nature of our human existence. The fundamental reason the vineyard is in a mess, He says, is that men and women, Jews or Gentiles or whoever they may be, habitually run away from that accountability. 'You can be a god too' the devil told Adam. And in his arrogance he believed the lie, and chose the path of moral defiance rather than moral obedience.

In this respect the Jews' rejection of the prophets is not essentially different from our human rejection of God generally. Paul argues that very point in his letter to the Romans. Deep down he says, we all know enough of our responsibility to God to submit our lives to His rule. The Jew has the Bible, the Gentile has his conscience. We are all without excuse. We are all sinners. We are all tenants in arrears with the rent. And that's why the owner intervenes in our lives. And when He does, that's why our immediate reaction, like the tenants, in the parable is not one of surprise but of resistance.

Jesus would surely have us realise that in our twentieth century exactly the same kind of illegitimate bid for moral autonomy that led to the failure of Israel is leading to the failure of our secular vision for a better world.

Here's the root of those ecological disasters of which the Green Party is constantly reminding us. Having thrown off our proper sense of stewardship for this world God has given us, we think we can do what we like with His creation, abusing it in any way with impunity.

Here is the cause of all those failed socialist dreams, of which the collapse of the Communist bloc is the most recent and tragic example. We human beings are just too greedy, too selfish, too lazy, too corrupt to make such utopian dreams of economic co-operation come true. Here is the spark from which the fire of revolutionary violence spreads its cruel terrorism around our world today, the resentment against authority which is convinced that somehow it's nobler and more dignified to blow up representatives of authority than to submit to them.

Here too is the soil from which the awful spectre of tyranny continues to haunt the human race, armed now with all the weaponry of psychological manipulation and computerised surveillance with which modern science has endowed it. We human beings have a power complex. Like an incompetent actor determined to play Hamlet, so puny man has ambitions to play God. And he is congenitally incapable of realising that the role is too big for him. So instead of giving power to humble men and women who might lead nations along the path of moderation and peace, again and again we invest power in the megalomaniacs, the Stalins, the Hitlers, the Saddam Husseins–and then winge at the leviathan of control and intimidation with which they encircle us and destroy our freedom.

It all comes down to the same thing. We are not content to be tenants of the vineyard. We insist on being owners. The ingratitude of it is bad enough: that God should bestow such privilege and dignity on the human race, such potential for creative endeavour, and that we should be so little prepared to render anything back to God. But it is the futility of it which is so pathetic. For it's a rebellion doomed to failure. The insane insolence of it, that puny creatures should wave their fists at omnipotence rejecting anything and everybody that God sends to remind us of the debt that we owe Him, and think that we'll get away with it! Surely He won't tolerate it!–Will He?

The extraordinary thing about Jesus' story is that He tolerates it for so long.

How Jesus understood His own mission

"What shall I do? I will send my son, whom I love; perhaps they will respect him" (20:13)

I find a pathos in verse 13 which is intensely moving. Jesus portrays here the patience of God, who has provided rebel human beings with one opportunity after another for repentance, only to find Himself slapped in the face every time. Yet still He desires to show His mercy; still He restrains His righteous indignation and turns the other cheek. He will offer one last chance, even if it means gambling with the most precious thing He has. 'My son, whom I love.'

But we must not allow the emotional power of those words to obscure their vital theological significance. I want you to remember again the demand that provoked this parable in the first place back in verse 2. 'Tell us by what authority are you doing these things. Who gave you this authority?'

It's hard to escape the conclusion that here in verse 13, Jesus is giving a straight answer to that question. 'I will send my son, whom I love.' In a remarkable way Jesus has introduced Himself as a character in His own story. If we have any doubts they are surely dispelled by the addition of that qualifying phrase, 'whom I love', because that's the very same word that came from heaven when Jesus was baptised by John back in Luke 3. 'You are my son, whom I love,' said the voice. The coincidence is just too great, especially when you recall that Jesus has just made a direct reference to the baptism of John in verse 3.

There is no missing Jesus' implied assertion in verse 13. The prophets who came before were servants of God. 'But I am different,' He says. 'I am special. I am the beloved Son.' I don't believe that the importance of that self-identification by Jesus can be exaggerated.

Especially so in our day. Let me tell you why. In the last thirty years or so, liberal theology in this country and indeed around the world has been conducting a relentless public campaign to discredit the doctrine of the deity of Christ. The whole idea of God having a Son who comes to earth in the shape of a man, they argue, is a fantastic fairy tale which no modern person can be expected to entertain any longer. John Robinson launched the first public salvo back in 1963 with the notorious *Honest to God*. Then came the Baptist, Michael Taylor, with a similar public statement in 1971. In 1977 we had the Anglican symposium entitled *The Myth of God Incarnate*. In 1984 one of the contributors, Don Cupitt, pushed the matter even more firmly into the public eye with his TV series 'The Sea of Faith'. Most recently of course the Bishop of Durham has kept the pot boiling with his newspaper interviews.

The reason for this academic conspiracy is not hard to

discern. It is the doctrine of the deity of Christ which more than anything else obstructs dialogue between Christianity and other faiths. And such dialogue comes close to becoming an obsession with many of our contemporary theologians and churchmen. Do you want to be rejected as a candidate for the Christian ministry in any of the mainstream denominations today? Tell the candidates panel that you want to see Moslem Asian immigrants in this country converted to Christ. That's all they need to hear.

If only they can rob Christ of His divinity, so He becomes one among many of servants of God rather than the 'only begotten Son' of the church's Creed, then the way is wide open for major rapprochement between Christianity and Islam, Christianity and Hinduism, Christianity and just about anything else. And the ecumenical dream of a single world religion can dawn.

And they insist that such a reinterpretation of the person of Christ is possible, even desirable. Why? 'Because,' say these scholars, 'Jesus would never have claimed deity. No, an alien God-incarnate identity has been superimposed upon Jesus of Nazareth by the Christians who came after Him. He would be highly embarrassed to hear us calling Him Lord and God.' The deity of Christ, they maintain, is an invention of the early church. It was never part of Jesus' own teaching. So, at least, liberal scholarship asserts.

But that I suggest to you is most certainly not the implication of this parable. On the contrary, Jesus here displays a clear sense of His own uniqueness. 'I am the Son,' He says– quite distinct from the servants, the prophets who came before.

For the son bears not just the divine word, but the divine likeness. The son comes not merely to represent the king, but to be the king. Jesus sees Himself as no accident of history. He comes with the most specific purpose of asserting the Father's territorial rights over His rebellious vineyard. He comes, in a word, as the Messiah, to inaugurate the long-heralded kingdom of God of which those prophets had spoken.

There's only one way to avoid the conclusion that Jesus entertained such an understanding of Himself. That is, to discard this parable as pure invention. And that, of course, is what the scholars do. They can't bear the thought that Jesus would have incorporated Himself into a parable in this way as the Son, so they insist that the story has been worked over by later Christians to such an extent that its original form is now totally lost to us. But frankly there are no grounds at all for such a dismissal of Luke's record. Only prejudice of a most gross and blinkered kind could persuade anyone to deny that Jesus is here confessing a most remarkable filial consciousness. 'I am the Son,' he says, 'not merely a rabbi, not even a prophet, I am the Son of God and it is by virtue of that divine Sonship that I exercise the authority in the temple of which you complain.'

Notice again, the wistfulness of that divine soliloquy in verse 13: 'perhaps they will respect him.' He says the same today, as He looks upon the church and upon the world. I know it is irritating to the modern liberal mindset to say that one religion is better than the other. In our pluralist generation all the pressures are upon us to paint Jesus in non-exclusive colours. A prophet, a philosopher, a guru, anything will do.

But flattering though such titles are, there's nothing unique about them. You can admire such people without following them. You can ignore them, if you wish, without cost. But Jesus will not allow us to damn Him with faint praise in that way. He claims to be God's last resort, His final word, His beloved Son.

There will be no dissidents in heaven. There will be nobody saying 'Three cheers for Mohammed.' If Jesus is right, and I'm sure He is, heaven is united by a single unanimous verdict: Jesus is Lord. And if that's so, we've got to listen to Him. We've got to respect His authority. We have no choice.

But the awful truth is, we didn't. And the extraordinary truth is, He knew we wouldn't. 'But when the tenants saw him, they talked the matter over. 'This is the heir,' they said. 'Let's kill him, and the inheritance will be ours.' So they threw him out of the vineyard and killed him' (20:14–15).

There are so many dimensions to the significance of the cross that we couldn't possibly encapsulate its full meaning in a few words. Perhaps that's why we have to make it into a visual symbol. But in this parable, Jesus is focusing down on one element that perhaps we often miss in our theologising about its significance. The cross, He says, is the ultimate insult. The cross is the supreme gesture of human contempt for the rule of God. The cross is the final snub that puts the lid on centuries of snubs that God has received from the human race. We could not appreciate nor even tolerate anyone who challenges us to admit the debt we owe, who calls us to recognise our accountability to our Maker. So we crucified Him.

At that point it's all too easy for you and me once again to shelter behind the fact that Jesus was directly addressing first-century Jews in this parable. 'Oh yes,' we can say. 'It was their fault. The Jews, the Romans, we all know how barbaric they were. The crucifixion was an appalling judicial murder, of course it was. Why, when I watched Ben Hur last Christmas, my eyes were wet with tears at the injustice of it all.' But no, we cannot isolate ourselves from blame in that way. To do so is not to engage with this parable as Jesus wants us to engage with it, but to run away from it. The whole point of what Jesus is saying is that we are tenants too. We were there when they crucified our Lord.

Some of us are with those Roman bureaucrats, some with those violent soldiers, some with that mindless crowd. But where are most of us? We are where I said we were yesterday, among the pharisees, so smug in our biblical orthodoxy we couldn't recognise the Christ Himself if He walked through the door.

Our hands were not the actual hands that drove the nails through Jesus' hands. But our hearts are wicked, rebellious and irresponsible enough to have done it. I suppose we can plead ignorance. Indeed Jesus pleaded it for us. 'Father, forgive them,' He said, 'for they do not know what they are doing' (Luke 23:34).

But this parable surely exposes the generosity of that prayer, and the shallowness of such an excuse. For if we crucified Him in ignorance, it was nevertheless culpable ignorance. Jesus insists, these tenants knew only too well who it was they were murdering. That's why they were doing it.

'This is the heir,' they said, 'let's kill him, and the inheritance will be ours.' So Jesus would have us realise that deep down at the most profound levels of our personal honesty, we too know who He is and we too know why we don't want Him in our lives. It is that obsessive desire for independence, that lunatic ambition to play god. 'I don't want any patronising deity interfering in my life. I want to do my own thing thank you very much, I want to be my own master. This is the heir, let's kill him and the inheritance will be ours.' We've all said it. And every time we say it we add our personal nail to those that held Christ to His cross.

And that brings us to the third section of this story, which is the most solemn and the most searching of all.

How Jesus understood the future

"What then will the owner of the vineyard do to them?"
(20:15)

Once again, in its initial reference verse 15 is a prediction of the way in which the Jews, by their rejection of the Messiah, forfeited their spiritual privileges to the Gentiles. Matthew puts it clearly in his version of this parable. 'The kingdom of God will be taken away from you,' he says, 'and given to a people who will produce its fruit' (Matt. 21:43). It's understandable that the Jewish audience were offended by such a comment, for such a prospect tore the stuffing out of all those messianic dreams of theirs. As patriots, they were looking forward to the kingdom of God. It would be a day of triumph for the Jewish nation. 'No,' says Jesus, 'not at all. The kingdom of God spells a day of national catastrophe for the Jewish nation.'

But just as it would be foolish of us to think the only wicked tenants in this world are Jews, so it would be an even greater folly to assume that they are the only people God is angry with in this world. No, it is with the solemn prospect of judgement to come that Jesus confronts all of us at the end of His story.

He confronts the visible church with that prospect, for if the leaders of Jerusalem forfeited the spiritual privilege of Israel to the Gentiles because they failed to honour and respect God's Son as they should, what will God do to those so-called theologians and clerics who in their zeal for inter-faith dialogue deny the uniqueness of Christ? Is it any surprise that the mainstream denominations of our nation are declining in membership and influence today? Is it any surprise that new Christian groups who are not embarrassed to own a divine Christ as their Lord are capturing the initiative in our land today?

George Carey is right when he talks of the next few years as critical for the Church of England, and indeed for all mainstream denominations. For there are clear signs that God is giving the vineyard to others under the very noses of the bishops. I'm just hoping that George Carey is courageous enough and honest enough to admit that it is the defections from the apostolic faith of the New Testament on the part of some of the bishops, which is largely responsible. The glory is departing from some of our mainstream denominations, because of undisciplined error in the most fundamental matter: the Lordship of Christ.

He confronts the nation of Britain too with this prospect of final judgement, I believe. For if Israel had known blessing from God's help over the centuries, so has this land of ours. For a thousand years Christianity has been the official faith of this land. We were delivered from paganism in the distant past, from Islam in the Middle Ages, from apostate Catholicism in the sixteenth century, from fascist and Marxist dictatorship in this twentieth century. God has spared this country politically in most remarkable ways, time and time again.

More than that, He has blessed this nation with preachers of extraordinary power and influence: godly men who have called us as a nation to place ourselves under the authority of God; martyrs who have died to bring us the Bible; evangelists who have spent their lives promoting revival. And there are churches and chapels in every town and village testifying to God's signal goodness to this land.

What then will God do to us if, in the face of all that blessing, this land today turns its back on its Christian heritage and embraces a secularism as godless in its immorality and pagan in its superstition as many nations that have enjoyed not a fraction of its privileges?

Is it any wonder that economic prosperity is drying up, that the crime rate soars, that international influence declines? Our world is littered with wrecks of great empires and nations of the past. There is nothing immortal about Great Britain.

But perhaps supremely for us here this morning we have to face the fact that Jesus confronts each of us as individuals with the prospect of final judgement, in these sobering and solemn words at the end of His story.

To us verses 17–18 may seem difficult, but to Luke's readers they made eminent sense. For Jesus is fusing together here three verses with which they were very familiar. The New Testament quotes them often. Perhaps they come to Jesus' mind here because they are all about stones. And in the Aramaic language He spoke, the word for 'stone' and the word for 'son' sound almost identical.

The first quotation is from Psalm 118, and speaks metaphorically of the construction of a house. The masons building the house discover an oddly shaped stone that won't fit in the wall. At first they discard it, but then when they get to the very top of the building they realise that this is just the piece of rock they need to complete the supporting arch, the brick without which the whole edifice would otherwise collapse – the chief cornerstone.

In its original setting this psalm applied the metaphor to the king of Israel on his return to Jerusalem after a successful military campaign. The pagan nations had treated the king of Israel with contempt, and they discarded him like a worthless pebble. But now God has vindicated His anointed one and exalted him over his enemies. So the stone the builders had rejected has become the capstone. It's the Lord's doing and it's marvellous in our eyes, they sang.

But to the Jews of Jesus' day this entire psalm was interpreted messianically. Indeed we encounter a chorus of it on the lips of the crowd as they welcome Jesus triumphantly into Jerusalem on Palm Sunday: 'Blessed is he who comes in the name of the Lord.'

So what Jesus is doing is pointing out the full implications of Psalm 118 to these so-called Bible students who were challenging Him. 'If, as you believe, this is a messianic proph-

ecy, then don't you see what it implies? It implies that the
powerful men of this world will repudiate the Messiah just as
those pagan nations repudiated the king of Israel of old. But
then God will lift Him to His rightful place of exaltation. My
story of the rejected son is confirmed in that scripture you
know so well, the scripture of the rejected stone.'

And before they can recover from this startling expository
insight, with a stroke of genius Jesus welds on two more
verses from Isaiah 8 and Daniel 2 which also speak about
stones. The Isaiah text cautions that if Israel does not trust
the Lord, then the Lord Himself will become like a stone
over which they stumble. The quotation from Daniel speaks
of a stone or a rock symbolising the kingdom of God which
will be used at the end of the age as a hammer in God's hands
to destroy all the opposing kingdoms of the earth and smash
them to smithereens.

And by fusing all these scriptures together, Jesus is issuing
a solemn warning. The stone the builders discarded, he says,
now lies on the ground. You are plotting to murder God's
son. Careless people stumble over Him to their destruction,
as Isaiah said they would. But one day soon He will be raised
up to the top of the arch. And for people who are foolish
enough still to reject Him then, it will no longer be them who
fall over Him, but rather he who falls on them, as Daniel
predicted. 'It is a dangerous thing,' He says, 'to reject Me.
You are playing with fire. Put yourself in the owner's place in
my story and you will realise why. Do you really think God is
going to tolerate the preposterous insolence of the human
race for ever? Do you think He will stand idly by and grant
His beloved Son no vindication in the face of His enemies?'

No, a day of accounting is coming. 'What you do with Me,'
He says, 'the Son, the Stone, will determine your final destiny on that day. You must choose either to be broken
voluntarily by Me, your rebellious pride humbled and chas-
tened by recognition of who I am; or you must choose to be
finally crushed by me, judged, condemned for your com-
plicity in this rebel world.' This is a solemn message. But it's
one that I fear as churches and preachers we are growing
reluctant to be frank about.

It's a great mistake to confuse divine patience with divine

indifference. According to this story God is being patient
with us human beings, sending one servant after another and
finally sending His own Son. The danger is, we could be
deceived into thinking that His patience is infinite. But Jesus
says it is not. The heart of God is unbearably provoked. You
must not mistake His patience for indifference.

It's popular to speak of God as a kindly old fellow, all
love, who would never harm a fly. But where have we got
that idea from? It certainly wasn't Jesus. It is only God's
moral indignation against evil that prevents His love from
degenerating into mere sentimentality. We don't really
admire people who are never angry. There are times when
righteousness demands anger, at cruelty, at prejudice for
example. We can't respect a person who remains in some
kind of insulated benignity when they are confronted by real
wickedness.

If there are times when people ought to be angry, how
much more then will there be a time when God will be angry!
Do not mistake impatience for indifference. He's patient
with us men and women, but not indifferent towards our sins.
We are accountable; and ultimately we shall give account of
that missing rent, account for those injured servants, account
for that murdered Son.

How does Jesus see the future? He sees it as a day of
accounting, a day of judgement.

Samuel Johnson remarked, 'I remember that my Maker
has said that He will place the sheep on His right hand and
the goats on His left. That is a solemn truth which this
frivolous age needs to hear.' The frivolous age he was talking
about was the eighteenth century, but there's plenty of fri-
volity still around.

It disturbs me most profoundly that so few people today
take hell seriously. Many of those theologians I mentioned
earlier are universalists, insisting that hell is a sub-Christian
superstition. 'Who can possibly imagine a loving God tolerat-
ing such an obscenity?'

More popularly, people joke about it. 'Well, if I go to hell
there'll be plenty of people who'll go with me' – as if hell were
going to be some jolly party for the society of the free spirits.
I do not deny that the language of judgement the Bible

sometimes uses is difficult. I sympathise with some, even among my evangelical brethren, who find the doctrine of hell confusing and unpalatable. I would agree that Jesus uses symbolical language when He speaks of 'hell-fire' and 'the worm that never perishes'. But I cannot believe He would use such language unless He wanted to warn us of something real and dreadful. And I cannot believe that the Son of God would have hung on the cross amid such agony if He did not want to spare us something even worse. Of course judgement is real. It's because judgement is real we need rescue. The very word 'salvation' would be meaningless if there was nothing to be saved from.

Here is a God, I say, who sees us as individuals walking into misery, determined to be what by very nature we cannot be; independent of Him. He puts up signposts in our path to warn us, He sends messengers to try and persuade us, but we despise and ignore them. He even sends His own Son, and He watches as we murder Him. Yet still He persists in urging us to come to our senses. Still He persists in urging us to discover our true human destiny in fellowship with Him as tenants of His world, not as usurpers of it.

But if we insist upon our autonomy He will give it to us. In that sense He doesn't have to send any of us to hell. Our tragedy is we are already walking there. The one principle of hell is, 'I am my own.' If we tell God to leave us alone, Jesus says, then at the end of the day that's just what He will do: leave us alone permanently. The Bible says it is a fearful thing to fall into the hands of the living God, but I'll tell you something that scares me even more. And that's falling out of His hands.

' "What then will the owner of the vineyard do to them? He will come and kill those tenants and give the vineyard to others." When the people heard this, they said "May this never be!" ' (20:15–16). Should not those words generate a great concern for holiness in us? Should they not generate a great passion for evangelism in us? Should they not generate in us a great seriousness about this Christian faith we affirm? And if there is here some dear friend who is backsliding from a faith in Christ you once professed, or uncommitted to Christ altogether, should those words not generate in you a great concern for your eternal destiny? What will He do with you?

Do you notice that phrase with which Luke introduces verse 17? 'Jesus looked directly at them,' it says. There's a strange intensity about that, isn't there. He fixes His eyes upon these people. What was in that look as He issues this solemn final warning to them. Urgency, pity, appeal–love? Yes, that surely more than anything. For these are the eyes which just a few hours before, had been weeping for Jerusalem.

Can we not then sense that Christ, at the end of our Convention, looks directly at us? He looks at us with that same intensity, that same urgency. All the love of God for us stupid, sinful, wayward men and women is concentrated in that gaze. For we were there, with all the other rebellious tenants, we were there when they crucified the Lord. We can't plead innocence. What was it Peter said? 'God has made this Jesus, whom you crucified, both Lord and Christ' (Acts 2:36).

'What shall we do?' they begged Him. And He replied, 'Repent.' If the eyes of Jesus are fixed on us this morning, you can be absolutely sure that is the response He expects from us too. We have insulted God, we have presumed upon His patience too long. We have despised His generosity too long. We have treated His Son as a second-class feature in our lives too long. He waits now, patiently, but not indifferently, for our apology, and for the payment of that long overdue debt of moral obedience we owe Him. He is not going to wait for ever.

THE ADDRESSES

WHILE WE WAIT

by Rev. Alistair Begg

Titus 2:11–14

If the vibrancy of our singing tonight is any indication of the expectancy of our hearts, then I can say with confidence that during this week God will surely fulfil the promise of His word: He will fill the hungry with good things.

Let me continue the metaphor of food by way of illustration. In America, and perhaps in Britain also, there are restaurants where the waiters do not only serve food but also perform. They might be bringing you a bowl of soup and suddenly burst into a solo from Gilbert and Sullivan or Rogers and Hammerstein. They may even produce eggs from their pockets and juggle them at your table. Perhaps this performance is meant to distract from the quality of the food that you're about to eat!

I mention this because what takes place in those restaurants has I believe also begun to take place in the church, where some who have been granted the awesome responsibility of opening the word of God have begun to believe that they have the responsibility not simply of carrying the food but of performing as well. Consequently preaching may become a spectator sport.

But as the first waiter–as it were–out of the kitchen this week, I want you to know that not one of us is able to take any credit for the food. All of us, to a greater or lesser degree, are responsible for the way it's arranged on the plate, but none of us are responsible for what happens to it once it's

been delivered to your table. And so we come free of the
burden of having to dress it up in any way. Indeed Paul tells
us in the first two chapters of Titus that Titus' responsibility
when preaching in his generation was to dish it out; it was the
responsibility of the listeners to dress it up. You'll find that
taught in 2:10: You should teach them in such a way about
God, says Paul, that in turn 'they will make the teaching
about our God and Saviour attractive'.

It would seem, looking at the book of Titus, that Titus
himself was concerned about what he should be preaching
and teaching. As we read chapter 2 it becomes apparent that
Paul too was concerned that his young son in the faith should
keep on track in this respect. Titus was working in an
environment not dissimilar to our own. Households were
being ruined by the wrong message being proclaimed by bad
messengers from dishonest motives. And so it's no surprise to
find Paul concerned about what should be taught.

In 2:1 he tells Titus, 'You must teach what is in accord with
sound doctrine.' There follows an extended section on the
practical application of this, and then in verse 15, at the end
of the chapter, he sums it all up saying 'These then, are the
things you should teach.' So some months ago, sitting in a
little room in Ohio looking for inspiration and encouragement for this opening evening, I decided that I would
respond to the exhortation of Paul to Titus. These are the
things that I want to teach this evening.

I want to encourage you by telling you that we're not going
to plough through all fifteen verses. We are going to look
through the 'eye' of verse 14. But we're not going to remove
verse 14 from its context. So we must remind ourselves that
those who were listeners to Titus and were the first readers of
this letter, were like us in that they were looking back:
looking back to the glorious appearing of 'the grace of God'
(verse 11) encapsulated in the birth, life, ministry, death and
resurrection of the Lord Jesus Christ (verse 13). Like us they
looked back to when God came in a moment in time, invaded
our time-space capsule, and revealed His grace in the person
of His Son.

That is an historic reality. But the church is not a church
that is simply looking back. As we read on, we discover that

it is a church that is looking forward. And it is looking forward to the appearing again of Jesus. The first time, He came surprisingly; unexpectedly; ignominiously. The next time, He will come surprisingly—and yet gloriously and transformingly. He will come. And the church here is described as a waiting church; in verse 13 Paul reminds Titus that whatever else we're doing, we're waiting.

The kind of waiting Paul is speaking of is not the kind of waiting motorists do in queues. Nor is it the kind of waiting that a wife does as she looks again and again at the clock expecting her husband home from the golf course. As the church of Jesus Christ we are 'the waiting ones', but we are to be waiting not lethargically or disinterestedly but expectantly.

The parables of Jesus made that perfectly plain. We're not to be like the five foolish virgins: we're to be like those who are wise and who are ready. We are to be responding to the hymn-writer who says: 'When the bridegroom cometh will your robes be white? Pure and white, in the blood of the Lamb?' Oh, that within our hearts we might genuinely sing,

Face to face with Christ my Saviour
Face to face—what will it be?
When with rapture I behold Him...

So that if we profess faith in Jesus Christ and somebody were to interview us walking from this tent tonight and ask us 'What are you about?', one of the things we would tell them is 'I'm waiting.'

'And for what?'

'Well, it's not so much for *what*. It is for *whom*.'

'Then, for whom?'

'For Christ...my Saviour.'

The waiting Christian is a Christian who is in no doubt about the motivation and incentive, firstly to be zealous in evangelism and secondly to be deadly serious about holiness. Augustine said that the person who claims to love the coming of the Lord is not the individual who says it is very near, nor is it the one who says it is afar, but it is he or she who, whether it be near or far, awaits it with all their hearts.

So Paul tells Titus to tell the others who are waiting that while they wait this is how they need to live.

That somewhat lengthy introduction leads us to verse 14, which I would like to summarise in three phrases: 'For us', 'For Him', 'For good'.

For us

First of all you will notice that this Jesus for whom we wait gave Himself for us. To the apostle Paul, this was no arms-length theology. You will recall that he not only said that the Lord Jesus loved us and gave Himself for us, but that he said the Lord Jesus loved *me* and gave Himself for *me*. And as Paul underscores this to Titus and Titus passes it on, and as we consider it in 1991, you will notice that there are two truths that emerge from it.

First is the truth that in Christ, we are *purchased*. Notice what he says: 'He gave himself for us to redeem us'. This runs throughout all Paul's theology. Galatians 1:4, He 'gave himself for our sins'; Ephesians 5:2, He 'gave himself up for us'. Peter says of us that we were once enslaved, that we were committed to an empty way of life. And then at just the right moment – as Paul says in Romans 5 – God sent Christ to be our Saviour. And if anything is true for us tonight this is true, that His death has purchased our redemption: a death which He underwent voluntarily, a death which was substitutionary, a death which was propitiatory.

The death of Jesus Christ was not something supplied in time to correct a defect in the system. From all eternity God planned to purchase your redemption. And tonight, in the midst of all that we know and all that we learn, we need to underscore these things.

I don't know how true it is in Britain, but it is certainly true in America that there is a significant drift towards what is called the holistic view. A holistic view of the gospel has developed. It's not entirely wrong, but it needs to be understood and it needs to be put in the context of this truth, that we are purchased.

The holistic view of the gospel makes it a springboard for

social action and political liberation, thereby giving the impression, whether it be in Keswick, London, Tokyo or Washington DC, that this is what the church is about. But the church is first of all about personal transformation. Jesus Christ came to be Saviour. 'And you will call His name 'Jesus' for He will save His people from their sins'... 'Unto you a child is born and unto you a son is given'... 'And He will be – Saviour.'

You may say to me, 'Do you really think that a group like this needs to underscore that?' Well, I hope it's not necessary; but I want you to do it. We do well to recognise that salvation involves more than our souls, but we dare not fall into the trap of believing that it involves less than our souls. At Crusaders in Scotland we used to sing a chorus from the CSSM chorus book that went like this:

He did not come to judge the world,
He did not come to blame;
He did not only come to seek,
It was to save He came...
And when we call Him Saviour
We call Him by His name.

The foundational truth upon which practical holiness must always be built is the fact that in Christ you are purchased. You're not your own; you were bought with a price. Therefore glorify God in your body.

Secondly, we are *purified*. Not purchased to sit on a shelf and be dusted, but to be redeemed from all wickedness and be purified for Himself. You will notice, incidently, that Paul does not suffer from the contemporary paranoia about negativity. He is very straightforward in saying that Jesus Christ gave Himself for us to redeem us 'from'. Earlier he has said 'The grace of God that brings salvation has appeared to all men' (verse 11). And now he has no problem about being 'positively negative': 'Titus, teach this. Tell the old men, the old women, the young girls and the young men that now they are in Christ, purchased to be purified.'

Not only are we redeemed from the lawlessness which marked us before; we are also cleansed from impurity. We are taught to say 'No' to ungodliness, to worldly passion; and we're taught to say 'Yes' to self-control, to righteousness and to godly living. Do you remember the Sunday School chorus?

> Learn to say no,
> learn to say no,
> to everything evil
> wherever you go.

Consumed by the notion that we must be positive, that nobody's self-esteem may be tampered with, we run the risk of missing this truth: that 'for us' means purchased–but it also means purified.

For Him

Not only did He give Himself 'for Us'; we are to be 'for Him'. Verse 14: He 'gave himself for us to redeem us from all wickedness and to purify for himself a people...' For us–we are purchased, we are purified. For Him–firstly, we are *planned*. God planned for us.

I believe that it was Alan Stibbs who in his commentary on 1 Peter said something like this: 'It is God's unmistakable purpose from all of eternity to have a people of his own. And it is the utterly undeserved privilege of the repentant sinner to be made part of that people.' If we were in any doubt about that, we need only listen to Jesus preaching. For example, in John 6, addressing a diminishing crowd, He lays it on the line about what it means to be a Christian: 'All that the Father gives me will come to me, and whoever comes to me I will never drive away' (6:37); 'And this is the will of him who sent me, that I shall lose none of all that he has given me, but raise them up at the last day' (6:39). That is Jesus preaching.

What about Jesus praying? 'Father, I want those you have given me to be with me where I am, and to see my glory' (John 17:24). Surely one of the great mysteries tonight is that any one of us is here. Don't you find yourself saying, 'How could it ever be that I could sing such a song as 'There is a redeemer, Jesus, God's own Son...When I stand in glory I will see His face'?'

There was no-one more surprised than Saul of Tarsus on the Damascus road, but God was not surprised. He said to

Ananias 'You get down there and do what I'm telling you, because this man is My chosen instrument, to bear My name before the Gentiles'. You are not here tonight, believer, haphazardly. You have not been purchased indiscriminately, God's purpose for your life is perfect, and it is bounded by the parameters of His eternal counsel and will. And it is that which gives us stability in the shifting sands of the changing world in which we live: He has planned to have a people for Himself.

> I know not why God's wondrous grace
> to me hath been made known;
> nor why, unworthy as I am,
> He bought me for His own.

Secondly, we are *peculiar*. Now, I'm not using an unusual version. I am using the word deliberately because I want you to know that in Christ tonight we are peculiar, in the sense that He purified for Himself a people *'that are His very own'*. We don't belong to anybody else; we belong to Jesus. We are, to use a sixties phrase, the Jesus People. Now the fact is tonight that in the streets of Keswick and in your office and in your surgery and in your supermarket, God's purpose for you is to be 'peculiar'. Some of us are doing a good job about being peculiar in the wrong way, but we are to be peculiar God's way.

It would be easy if He just gave us all a big plastic nose and sent us out in the street. Then people would say 'Oh yes, we know the Christians. They're the ones with the plastic noses!' But He decided not to do it that way. Instead, the peculiarity would be internally motivated and externally revealed. You and I will never be peculiar for Jesus' sake until we have peculiar minds, peculiar hearts, peculiar desires, peculiar motives. Jesus is in the business of making us 'peculiar'.

Until a teenager realises that (I speak from experience), they will never be effective for God in their school. Until a businessman understands that, he will never stand for Christ in his daily routine. Until a lady is prepared to be thought peculiar by her peers, she will never live effectively to the glory of God. And tonight as we read these verses, and as we realise that we were purchased, purified and planned, we've got to face the fact that He meant us to be 'peculiar'.

Indeed He underscores it again and again. Titus 3:3–once we lived in malice and in envy and we were hated and we hated one another, but all of that is changed now. You'll find the same thing when you read Ephesians 4.

Now this is all straightforward stuff, isn't it? So why take time to reinforce it?

I'll tell you why. Because the constant refrain that I hear is of the church at pains to tell the world that we're no different from it: 'We're just like you.' Well, we're like the world in its need, but we're not to be like the world in its sin. And the danger is that we become like it in its sin and so we have nothing to say to it in its needs. Many of us were brought up in the 1950s and early 1960s, understanding 'Learn to say no, learn to say no.' Then we got all liberated and decided we had to move the pendulum to the centre. Unfortunately we weren't smart enough to move it to the centre and now we've moved it right out to the other side.

So now we say 'Learn to say yes, learn to say yes'. Can I be a Christian and do this? Can I be a Christian and do that? Can I be a Christian and do something else? Every time we say that, we're seeking to justify something which we know in our conscience is probably debatable.

Peculiarity. The peculiarity of integrity in a shady world; the peculiarity of reality in a cardboard world; the peculiarity of purity in a dirty world. One of the Reformers said 'If we live like the wicked it's because we are wicked.'

Islam knows nothing of our diffidence about being peculiar. Some time ago, travelling in New York State, we pulled into a petrol station. As we did so I noticed a group of people behind the petrol station. They arranged themselves in order and knelt down, once they had found where the East was. And they conducted their prayer-time there as the world drove by on Highway 90. People went by and said 'That's peculiar!' But the Moslem didn't care. And the Christian's not supposed to care. Do you care?

For Good

'For us', He came and purchased us, that we might be purified. 'For Him' we live, planned and peculiar. And 'For good'?

Since we already have four 'p's we might as well have another two. Here they are.

First, we are to be *practical*. Paul has emphasised this all the way through. Back in the beginning of the chapter he's given practical instruction concerning family life, concerning the market-place of our days. In 3:1 he wants them to be ready to do whatever is good. In 3:8 he says 'Make sure that you tell them to be careful to devote themselves to doing whatever is good', because that is how these individuals will be distinguished from those who claim to know God and yet by their actions deny Him. 'They claim to know God, but by their actions they deny Him. They are detestable, disobedient and unfit for doing anything good' (1:16).

What a disaster! To claim to know God, and yet to be useless for God. Recently I could not understand why our air-conditioning at home wasn't working, though it had been switched on all night. You could hear the noise of the unit, but it wasn't cooling. So eventually I had a look at it and discovered that there was enough power to rotate the fan, but not enough to activate the cooling unit. So we had all the right noises, but none of the transformation we were looking for.

Loved ones, you and I know that to put our bodies on the seats in this place is no guarantee either of knowing God or of living for Him, of being sold out to Him. There will be people in this tent during these days who will make all the right noises, without any real change.

We are to be practical: and finally we are to be–*passionate*. We're not only to do what is good, we're to be eager to do what is good. The word there is translated 'zealous, devoted'. We are to say 'No' to worldly passions, he tells us, but we're not be passionless. What a tragedy a passionless church is–insipid and bland, when Jesus said we are to be involved and bold! How do you get insipid and bland churches? You fill them with insipid and bland Christians; and there they sit.

I'm just reading J. I. Packer's latest book, *A Quest for Godliness*. In it, he says that the reason we need the Puritans at this point in the twentieth century is for one reason: because they show us a warm-hearted compassion with a clear-minded passion.

Can I ask you tonight, are you passionate about God? Are you passionate about the fact that He purchased you? That He planned for you? That He made you peculiar? That He wants you to go out and be practical? Are you passionate about it–or is it just another event? There is little fear of us being thought drunk on the streets of Keswick until we find ourselves filled with the same power that put the Christians on the streets of Jerusalem.

'For us', we were purchased, to be purified. 'For Him', He planned, for us to be peculiar. 'For good', that we might be practical and that we might be passionate. Let's see some passion for God, in our day! God give us again the spirit of C. T. Studd: 'If Jesus Christ be God and died for me, then no sacrifice that I could ever make for Him would ever be too great.'

THE INDWELLING CHRIST

by Dr Luis Palau

Studies in Galatians

Tonight, at the stage that we are in the Convention, we want
to talk about the forgiveness of sins. Some of you have been
meditating on failure, on the cloud hanging over your head;
perhaps over the last few months you've had areas where the
Holy Spirit is pointing the finger and you feel a great burden
of guilt.

We just sang the glorious hymn,

And can it be, that I should gain
An interest in the Saviour's blood?
Died He for me, who caused Him pain,
For me who Him to death pursued?

—and then the last verse:

No condemnation now I dread,
Jesus and all in Him is mine...

And if anybody is hurting tonight, and you feel despised,
even rejected by the Lord: my dear brother and sister, if you
open your heart to Christ—whether at six-and-a-half, as Dr
Kendall has told us he did, or much later in life—the Lord has
forgiven you if you're repentant. Amen?—it's true! The blood
of Jesus cleanses from how many sins? *All* sins. You're sure?
Amen!

And Scripture says it's continuous; the blood of Christ

continues to cleanse us from all sin. Therefore, there is no condemnation. Therefore, if you have confessed your sins you are forgiven. Now listen to the rest. You must leave the past behind, and, cleansed by the blood, confess before the Lord and you are free. Your conscience, your heart, should be free. How does that verse go?

> I woke, the dungeon flamed with light.
> My chains fell off, my heart was free,
> I rose, went forth and followed Thee.

Perfectly biblical truth! And tonight I pray, as we look to the future now, that you've settled that sin, whatever it may be, that you've left it at the foot of the cross, that you've accepted by faith: 'Lord Jesus, Thy blood has cleansed me from all sin, therefore my conscience is clean–praise God! And I am free, the chains have fallen off, therefore I don't have to keep dwelling on the past, I don't have to keep beating my breast, I don't have to think that I'm humble by being reminded of my sins.'

The Bible says 'God takes our sins and casts them at the bottom of the sea.' Corrie ten Boom used to say 'And then He puts up a sign saying 'No fishing allowed'.' The Lord says 'Your sins and evil deeds I remember no more'–praise God! And as far as the East is from the West, so far He removes our transgressions from us. Other people may remember, but the Lord says 'I don't.' And therefore, we don't have to remember.

It's not that you forgive yourself. That's an unbiblical idea, I don't know who invented it. But God has forgiven you. You accept that forgiveness and go on free–free–free by the cross and the blood of Jesus Christ. Are you there tonight? Then let's move on to the next step.

Let's go to Galatians 1:15–17. You may remember that every chapter of Galatians speaks about the indwelling Jesus Christ. And this is the secret of true freedom on a daily basis for the believer: the indwelling life of the resurrected Lord Jesus Christ.

Those of us who were here this morning and had the Bible study with our brother R.T. Kendall will remember that the Lord really spoke to us. Especially through such words as

Jacob's 'The Lord is in this place and I was not aware of it.' Now the Lord is in this place tonight. Are you quiet enough in your mind and your heart that you are aware of His presence?

I like the little word, when Martha and Mary had lost their brother and some people came from outside the village; they said to Mary and Martha 'The Master is here...and He's calling for you.' And you know, my dear brothers and sisters, we are in the middle of this Convention and the Master is here and He's calling for you. I hope we can forget all about everybody else, even husband and wife, for a moment tonight, and take it personally.

The Lord this morning said to us that Jacob was wrestling with God. Most of us have wrestled with God. It's actually not a good thing to do but we all do it. Wrestling with God, in a sense, is rebellion, isn't it? We ought to be able to say, 'Lord, what is it? I'll do it'...'What did You promise? I believe it'...but we are stubborn. And that's why the work of the cross, the work of the Holy Spirit, goes on from beginning to end of our Christian life, and only when we get to heaven it's finally over.

But Jacob was wrestling with God for a good reason. He wanted God to bless him. And in that sense perhaps it was a good kind of wrestling. It was asking God 'Bless me, Lord. Bless me Lord. Bless me Lord.' Jacob knew that he was a schemer, he was a cheat, he wanted the blessing but he went about it wrong. And if you were here on Sunday night you might remember that the Galatians were in that very same situation. They wanted the fullness of God, they wanted spiritual success: but they were going about it wrong. The Galatians wanted a super-life-style, the fullness of the Holy Spirit, they wanted to be powerful for God–but they were going about it wrong. That's what Jacob was doing too. They wanted to please God but they went about it in a mistaken way.

Dr Kendall and I have talked about it quite a bit this week. We believe that the teaching that God has emphasised in this Convention, and in all the years back, is fundamental for the believer and for the church of God all over the world.

Because most of us have made the same mistake as the Galatians.

In the last few days I've talked to several people, mostly youngish men as it happens. They expressed a feeling of deep frustration and fruitlessness in their Christian lives, of an absence of the assurance of the indwelling Christ. And for me all their statements reflect the feeling of many brothers and sisters in Jesus Christ who somehow have yet to find the freedom that there is in Jesus Christ. Most of us have gone through periods searching for it. Our prayer is that tonight many of you will come to understand it, when you understand what Paul says here in chapter 1.

The indwelling Christ becomes real to us at conversion

At conversion, says Paul, He 'called me by His grace, was pleased to reveal his Son in me' (1:15–16). When we were first converted most of us didn't understand much of doctrine, but almost all of us felt 'Ah! Now I have Jesus Christ. Now I am forgiven. Now I have eternal life. Now I'm going to heaven.' And we were thrilled beyond words. And for those first days, weeks, months – in some cases years – there's that first excitement and love because we've understood the Lord Jesus Christ.

We couldn't put it into clear words. In some cases the motivation wasn't the highest – in mine it was very, very untheological: I didn't want to go to hell. I know it's a low-class reason for being converted. And from that day I was happy that I had eternal life. I didn't understand the indwelling Christ, it took me many years to really understand it. But in that first moment I knew that Christ had been revealed in my heart, that I had eternal life.

Paul adds 'to reveal His son in me, so that I might preach Him...I did not consult any man.' Dr Kendall this morning was teaching us about having a faith of your own, about knowing the living Christ yourself and enjoying it. The first thing is, by faith, to truly understand the indwelling presence of Christ and to reject legalism, formalism and all outward appearances of Christianity in favour of the reality that the risen Christ lives in my heart. That's the first step. It actually takes place at conversion. In a sense we hardly knew it was happening, most of us, but it happened. The moment we received Jesus Christ, the moment we trusted Him, the moment we repented and believed in Him–Christ came into our lives.

What a glorious thing that is! Affirm it and accept it! You may not 'feel' His presence right now, but the fact is that if you repented and believed in the Lord Jesus He lives in your heart.

Jesus Christ came into our hearts to give us life

The secret of daily living, by the indwelling Christ, is found in Galatians 2:19–21. First we established, or the Holy Spirit establishes, that Christ came into our hearts the moment we were converted. Now comes daily living. You know, brothers and sisters, one of the points I'd like to encourage you to think about is that Jesus Christ came into our hearts to give us life, life, life. Not so much duty, though duty comes later. He came to give us life.

You remember what He said? 'I have come that they might have life, and that they might have it more abundantly' (John 10:10 AV). That's the purpose of His coming. Not that we should be frightened, tight-lipped, tied up in knots, but rather that we should be set free by His indwelling resurrected life to really live life and enjoy it.

'The fruit of the Spirit is love, joy, peace' (Gal. 5.22). All three are emotions. They're well-based emotions–based on the solid rock of the cross and His indwelling presence, and our unity with God Himself. And 'against such there is no law'. Once on the radio I heard a speaker say 'There is no law against too much love and joy and peace. You can have all the love and joy and peace that you can have.' That's living! The apostle says here, 'I have been crucified with Christ and I no longer live, but Christ lives in me' (2.20).

Norman Grubb once wrote a booklet entitled *The Key to Everything*. That key is our union with the Lord Jesus Christ, because when you and I understand that we are crucified to the law, we are dead to legalism, to outward forms, to any empty ritualism that is devoid of the life of Christ–then we're alive. And when we allow the indwelling Christ to take over, when we intelligently begin to understand what it means that

Christ lives in me, what a marvellous deliverance that is! For some of us it takes us a long time to understand. But some get it quickly, and how blessed they are. Have you understood that Christ lives in you?

Paul says very plainly at the outset that the context is not only one of justification but also of sanctification. For 'by observing the law no-one will be justified' (2:16) and therefore by observing the law neither is anybody sanctified. That's why in chapter 3, you remember, he says 'You started by the Spirit and now you're going to end up with the flesh.' What a contradiction. You started life by being born of the Spirit and now you're going to pretend to do it by sheer fleshly determination? 'No way,' says the apostle Paul. But what does it mean to be crucified with Christ?

I have to admit that it took me a long time to understand how it works out. I went to conventions like this and meetings in my church with intensity, ever since I was seventeen and a half. That's why I'm so happy there are so many young people here; young people want to be holy and victorious just as much as we who are getting on in years.

I looked at many passages and my question was always 'What do they mean when they say that?' In 2 Corinthians 4:11–12 Paul says that the death of Christ is at work in us, so that the life of Jesus may be revealed in our mortal flesh. I used to sit for hours pondering: 'What does it mean, 'the death of Jesus at work in me'? How do I 'die'? What does it mean to 'die'?'

Another verse we've heard a thousand sermons on–'Take up your cross, deny yourself and follow Me' (see Luke 9:23). How do you 'take up your cross' and 'deny yourself'? I would be willing to do anything to enjoy the fullness of everything that God has for me. But how?

Another parallel verse about the 'grain of wheat' (John 12:24). I used to think to myself 'How do I rot, so that I can bring life?' I never got the picture. After years of trying to understand I came up with this: that what it means for me in July 1991 for the death of Jesus to be at work in me, for me to take up my cross, for the grain of wheat to fall into the ground and die, to be crucified with Christ, is this. Every time my will crosses God's revealed will and I choose God's revealed will over against my will, that is the death of Jesus at work in me. That is taking up my cross. That is the grain of wheat falling into the ground and dying. That is being crucified with Christ.

Yes, you make a big decision, we've all done it I'm sure; in our youth, middle age or whenever, perhaps at a camp or a convention like this one when there's a call to surrender; and as far as you know you've presented your body a living sacrifice, your all is on the altar, you've held nothing back. And if you were like me you thought 'Oh boy, I've made it now. There isn't anything left to put on the altar. It's all given over to the Lord.'

And yet a few days, or weeks later at most—hours perhaps—suddenly you stumble again and you fall back into some of your old habits. And you say 'What's going on? How many times do I have to lay it on the altar? How many times do I have to take a step forward?' Then I began to understand. You have to do it, my dears, every time till kingdom come. Every time that my will crosses God's revealed will and I choose His revealed will over against my will, that is the death of Jesus at work in me.

It might be in relation to some special sin. Every time it comes back you have a choice. And the beauty of knowing the resurrected Lord Jesus is that we are free to choose. You see, the unbeliever is not free to choose, because his will is still bound to sin. It has never been set free. But, the Bible teaches in Romans 6, our will has been set free, so that now by the Holy Spirit we have a choice. Every time that our will crosses God's revealed will, we can choose.

And we have the power of the indwelling Spirit to choose. It can go all the way from negative sins—sexual temptation, temptations of the tongue, whatever your temptation may be—to positive things, like opportunities.

My wife and I feel that one of the times we have to pick up the cross again and again and choose His will over against ours, is when we have to be parted from each other for a long time. I tell you it's painful to say goodbye to your wife. We'll have been married thirty years in about two weeks. We've four sons. And you know, you love your wife, you love your boys when they're babies and on till they're big fellows. And you want to be home and by nature you want to stay with them, or at least take them with you, but it's not possible– and yet you know the Lord wants you to go and proclaim the gospel, so you do it.

You may say, 'That's not a big problem.' It's big when you've done it 550 times and there's another 500 to go, and you know it. You kiss her goodbye and it's painful. Sometimes you weep. And it doesn't get easier, it gets harder in fact. But you do it again, and again and again. I hope that helps you, because I believe it gives an understanding of what it means.

Yes, on the cross we were crucified with Christ. In God's eyes you and I died there. But on a daily basis it happens every single time my will crosses God's revealed will and I choose His revealed will over against my will. That is the death of Jesus at work in me so that the life of Jesus is revealed in me. And the moment I make that choice I'm free, there's an exhilaration. That's why he says in 2.20, 'I no longer live, but Christ lives in me.' So, if you're tempted, the moment you make the choice you know you've broken the power of temptation, don't you? And when it's an opportunity to serve, you obey.

Now, the third step, and we'll come back to some application.

How to live the life indwelt by Jesus Christ.

In verses 3:26–27 we have the absolute equality, for all Christians, of the fullness of Jesus Christ. I won't dwell on this because it seems obvious, but I want some of you who are new babes, or who perhaps might be overawed by well-known teachers and preachers, to note that it says you are all children and sons of God through faith. All of you were baptised into Christ, have clothed yourselves with Christ. There is no difference.

This is not some high quality of life for some very distinguished missionary women and preacher men and evangelists and theological professors. This is for the tiniest and smallest believer. It is for everyone who knows Jesus Christ. It isn't a quality of life for only a few after many years of agony, or for missionaries because they are so sacrificial and they've left everything to go to some other part of the world. It's for everybody.

I hope we all believe it. But you'd be amazed: some of you young people may say 'Well, one of these days I'll get there'... No, no, no! Today! Today!–if you first of all say 'Lord, You've revealed Your Son in me. Now I'm committed to the way of the cross. I want to learn to be crucified every time my will crosses God's will. Lord, I commit myself to Your will over against my will.'

When you say that, the life of Christ begins to flow, though you don't even notice it most of the time. And the Lord begins to use you and to bless other people through you. You may not be aware of it till somebody has the love and courtesy to come and tell you. 'You know, you really blessed me'... 'Your prayer touched me'... 'When you gave me that word it helped me'... or whatever. They come and tell you, and you say 'Oh, that's wonderful! How did it happen?' You were not aware of it. It's the life of Jesus at work in you. It's the Christ who indwells you, at work through your life.

And you know, here it says that we are 'baptised' into Christ. What a phrase that is! Most of you know that *baptizo* in the Greek means to 'submerge'; that's what it means to be indwelt by Christ. We are submerged into Christ, we are baptised into Him. There is total union, total saturation so to speak. 'Anyone united to the Lord'–listen to this–'becomes one spirit with Him' (1 Cor. 6:17).

That took me a long time to understand. I always had a feeling myself that the Lord was way up there, distant, and I was down here; and that when I wanted to deal with the Lord–until I understood all this–I had to make a long-distance phone call. And then a brother helped me to understand. He said 'Look, do you really believe that Christ indwells you?' I said 'Yes.' He said 'Are you enjoying the fact, day by day?' I said 'No, and I want to.' He said 'Let me give you a little help to start every day.'

I was intrigued, you see, by this: 'You have clothed yourselves with Christ' (3:27). Did you notice that? First it says we are baptised into Christ–that's the work of God, it simply means confirming what God has already done. We are bap-

tised into Christ, we are submerged into Christ. We're united
with Christ. But then it says 'Clothe yourselves with Christ.'

And this brother said 'Watch how you pray each morning
when you get up. I expect you pray this way: "Oh Lord, here
we go again, it's Monday. Awful bunch at the office. Lord, I
can't stand the place. Help me to overcome another eight
hours with those people. Lord, I don't have what it takes.
Lord, give me strength. Lord I'm so weak—I know I'm going
to fail. I've been to church on Sunday and I was so happy, but
I know what those dirty guys are going to be talking about.
Oh Lord help me," and you wail and...' And I said 'That's
right.'

'And then you say "Lord, today I'll probably have an
opportunity to witness but I don't know what to say. Oh Lord
help me to do it right." And you wail and wail and you
already depress yourself with your own prayer.'

But then he said, 'Do you believe that the risen Christ
indwells you? Yes! Of course you do. So in the morning,
even before you hit the ground, say "Thank you Lord Jesus,
that You're alive today—and You're alive in me—I got to go
to that crummy office, but You're coming with me Lord and I
know that You promise to give me everything I need for this
day, because You said 'I am with you always'. All Your
resources are my resources. All Your joy is my joy. All Your
power is my power. Lord, I am very slow to witness but if an
opportunity comes You're going to remind me of the verses.
You're going to help me with the arguments. Thank you
Lord. It's going to be a good day." '

Now, that's different from positive thinking. Positive
thinking is just selling yourself on an idea. This is grounded
on truth and reality. Amen? Yes. The living Christ indwells
you. You're not 'selling' yourself on the hope that this is
going to happen, this is possible because the Lord has said 'I
am with you. I am in you. Now go in my power.'

So you thank Him for what He is going to do in you and
through you today. And notice, it says 'Clothe yourselves
with Christ.' The Holy Spirit doesn't use pictures for nothing.
I feel that the teaching here is that every morning, as soon as
you wake up, by faith you clothe yourself with Christ once
again. And you're saying 'Lord Jesus, I'm not going to face

the world alone, I am clothed by Yourself. Lord, by faith, I dress up with Yourself. I'm going out there Lord, with Your uniform on. I am not going alone. I am not alone. 'I'll never leave you'–'I'll never forsake you'–'I'm with you always, even to the end of the age'. I am united to Christ.'

This is a truth that is so practical and real! And if you are discouraged today, or feel that you don't know how it works, I pray that you will do it. Because, you know, the scripture says 'We are free to choose the will of God over our will. We are free to be happy. Therefore you can either start today with a very gripey spirit or you can get up and say "Lord Jesus, You indwell me, I am a temple of the Holy Spirit, I am a child of God, I am not just one of the others, I belong to Your family; and this day, by faith, I choose to be happy. Because Jesus Christ indwells me."

That's reality, brothers and sisters! That's what set me free. And I don't think I'm crazy. Because it's been going on for thirty years or more, and I can testify that it's really the presence of Jesus which works.

Don't go back to the old ways

Now we must move on quickly to chapter 4. And in verse 19 you find a little parenthesis: 'My dear children, for whom I am again in the pains of childbirth until Christ is formed in you, how I wish I could be with you now and change my tone, because I am perplexed about you!'

The Galatians had regressed. They had gone back. They had come out of ritualism and law and slavery, and now they were freed, by Jesus Christ who had been betrayed and crucified, by the Holy Spirit who'd come into their lives. Chapter 3 asks: He who worked miracles among you, did He do it by faith or by works?–obviously by faith. But now they're going back. Evidently the Galatians had not understood the indwelling life of Christ.

And if a person doesn't understand the indwelling life of Christ that is the temptation; to go back to the old ways. Some go back to the world and the fear of man. They say 'Look, this is so boring, it doesn't work, so I'm going back to the world. Listen, at least those guys have fun when they have a pint or two. But we sit here glumly, and we don't have any power or joy or freedom.' So they go back to the world. Others go back to legalism. 'No, I'm going to go back to a real religious atmosphere, where they have rules and regulations and tough leaders who tell you what to do and what not to do. At least it's comfortable there.'

You see many Christians do that. Where they don't understand the indwelling Christ they often fall into the hands of cults or strange little groupings of people who lose the joy, who are obviously grim and bitter and tight-lipped and beady-eyed, and they go around like the Secret Police checking everybody. No joy, no freedom. That's why people say 'If that's Christianity, keep it! The whole lot!' But it isn't Christianity, is it? It isn't. Oh yes, there's self-discipline, but that's very different from legalism.

Others go back to the tyranny of the flesh. They remember the old days, or inner temptations, and they say 'Hey, hey, hey! There is no joy here, there is no happiness, this is unacceptable. At least when you go with the flesh you have kicks even if it doesn't last long–but while it lasts, it lasts. And I'm going back to it.' And so you see Christians dropping out and going back into the fleshiest ways and into the most awful sins.

And so Paul says here–look at it again–'I am again in the pains of childbirth until Christ is formed in you.' Because the end result of understanding the indwelling Christ is that you become, slowly but surely, more and more like the character of Jesus Christ. It's not that you're perfect–only in heaven. But, as the years go by, we who understand the indwelling Christ really are being changed and transformed almost unawares from one degree of glory to another.

Hopefully our spouse, our old friends will notice it. But the fact is that Christ is being formed in us. And that's the objective: that we be formed into the image of His son. It happens gradually. Some of us expect instant maturity. Impossible! All Scripture teaches that we mature step by step by step. But the problem for the Galatians was, they had gone right back. Some to the world, some to the worst of the flesh, some to legalism. And therefore they were losing the whole thing. And now Paul says 'Oh my dear children, I worked so hard among you. I want Christ to be formed in you again, so to speak. You have to go back.'

And today, this morning, the Lord spoke to us when through Jacob we heard the message 'Go back to Bethel, go back to Bethel, go back to Bethel.' And dear brothers and sisters, if you're here tonight having known better days, when you were happy, you were joyful, you were filled with the Spirit and knew it; when you were free, without fear of anybody, not walking in the flesh – and you knew it; you were not in the world, for sure! – but you've gone back...Come back to where you started from. Come back and let Christ be formed in you again. Don't feel that because you understood it at one point and then you slipped back that it's all over, that you've gone too far, that the Lord has rejected you.

Rather say 'Lord Jesus, I'm coming back. I really want to be filled with Christ again.' And you know, it's a marvellous thing, He is very patient and very kind. And the Lord will work in your soul.

FIRSTBORN OF CREATION

by Dr John Balchin

Colossians 1:15–17

It's my conviction that many Christians begin the story of Jesus far too late on. They begin with Bethlehem and His wonderful birth, then go on to talk about His life, and then His death for sinners and His glorious resurrection. But in the New Testament you have a series of incredible statements made by Paul and others which take the story back before creation, before time began. And this is one of them, here in Colossians 1:15, where Paul speaks about Jesus not only as the image of the invisible God but also as 'the firstborn over all creation'.

It's a title that's frequently been misunderstood and misquoted. There are some who have used it to argue that Jesus was the first act of God's creation, that He was the first creature, if you like, to come into existence. That's the sort of interpretation that our Jehovah's Witness friends would like us to adopt. But it can't mean that, because Paul goes on to tell us what it does mean in verse 16: 'For by him'–better, 'in him'–'all things were created'. As all things were created in Him, that excludes the one in whom they were all created, doesn't it? In Him all things were created, and they were all created by Him and they were all created for Him.

It's interesting how often in these verses that little phrase 'all things' occurs. In fact in six verses it occurs five times. 'All things' means 'everything that there is'. Literally, all things– all creatures, all people, all spiritual beings, the lot; the universe and everything that the universe contains, everything you can see and a lot more you can't see. Think of the biggest thing you can think of, the furthest galaxy light-years away. Think of the finest detail, the microscopic organisms, the atomic structures, the very heart of this universe. All these are part of the 'all things', and Paul says all these things were created first of all 'in him'—not, as the New International Version translates it, 'by him'.

It's a very difficult idea to get hold of, isn't it. How could all things have been created in Christ? Well, the answer is of course to go to the rich Old Testament background that Paul and others were drawing upon when they taught about the relationship between Jesus Christ and creation. Back in the Old Testament you had the prophets and priests and men of wisdom who were in a class all of their own. They were men who asked questions like: What is the meaning of life? Why do the innocent suffer? What is the nature of the universe? And when these wise men asked, 'How did God create the world?', the answer was: in His wisdom.

It's obvious, isn't it, when you look at the world: a world so overwhelmingly intricate, so finely balanced, that it's difficult to avoid the idea that behind it is divine intelligence, a divine mind far beyond our own.

So in the Old Testament, creation is linked with wisdom. In other words it's saying: Look at the world as it is, isn't God clever? We see His wisdom. And as the Old Testament authors pondered on this idea under the guidance of the Holy Spirit they began to speak about wisdom in highly poetic terms, to the point where wisdom is spoken of not just as an idea but as a person—and as a person actually working alongside God in creation.

The most wonderful of such passages begins in Proverbs 8:22. There Wisdom speaks, as Wisdom does speak of course in the Book of Proverbs, as you know. 'I was the craftsman at his side. I was filled with delight day after day, rejoicing always in his presence, rejoicing in his whole world and delighting in mankind.' That's poetry—but what poetry!

The theme was taken up between the Testaments—a very important period if you are going to understand your New Testament, because the sort of things that were written between the Testaments were the sort of things that Jesus and the Apostles were aware of and read about. Between the Old Testament and the New, Jews pondered on this whole idea of God's wisdom; they began to explore the relationship between God and His world.

What they were doing was providing ready-made tools for people like Paul when they later came to explain who Jesus was. Actually, I don't think we realise, until we read those authors of the inter-testamental period, just how much the New Testament authors were claiming for the Lord Jesus Christ. In that time there were so many disparate ideas, themes, hopes and aspirations; but when you come to the New Testament they all come together and they focus on Jesus Christ. And that includes this rather enigmatic idea of wisdom.

How did they associate Jesus with wisdom? Well, if you read the Gospels carefully you will find there are references where Jesus drops hints that He knew He was the Wisdom of God. He gives us certain clues. But it was when the writers, under the Spirit's inspiration, pondered on God's purpose, that they understood that all God's intelligent purpose comes to focus in Christ. As Eternal Son, He perfectly and finally reveals the Father's mind.

So you have Paul writing to those ever-so-clever people at Corinth: 'Christ Jesus, who has become for us wisdom from God' (1 Cor. 1.30). Or later on in this letter to the Colossians: 'In whom are hid all the treasures of wisdom and knowledge' (Col. 2:3). But as we have seen in the Old Testament, the Wisdom of God is linked with creation–so if Jesus is the Wisdom of God, somehow He must be involved in creation: not merely born at Bethlehem and dying on the cross and rising on the third day. And this leads in the New Testament to a series of breathtaking statements about the Lord Jesus Christ.

'In the beginning was the Word, and the Word was with God and the Word was God. He was with God in the beginning. Through him all things were made; without him nothing was made. In him was life, and that life was the light of men' (John 1:1–4). There it is! 'In the past God spoke to our forefathers through the prophets at many times and in various ways, but in these last days he has spoken to us by his Son, whom he appointed heir of all things and through whom he made the universe. The son is the radiance of God's glory and the exact representation of his being, sustaining all things by his powerful word' (Heb. 1:1–3). There it is! 'He is the image of the invisible God, the firstborn over all creation. For by him all things were created: things in heaven and on earth, visible and invisible . . . all things were created in him [by him] and for him (Colossians 1:15–16).

A little while ago a number of Christadelphians started coming to our church. They were very sincere people, dissatisfied with their own church, and seeking. I talked with one of them–a man who had two theological degrees. And he explained the Christadelphian understanding of the Lord Jesus Christ. 'We don't believe in adoptionism,' he said. 'We don't believe that Jesus was just a man. We believe that He was begotten as Son of God when He became incarnate at Bethlehem.' It was what we would call an Economic Trinitarian view.

I asked him, 'How do you deal with those verses in Scripture which speak of Jesus Christ's activity before the creation of the world?' He replied, 'Well, He was in the mind of God from all eternity'. I responded, 'But it says much more than that, doesn't it: Jesus Himself said much more than that.'

Do you remember the upper room? 'And now, Father, glorify me in your presence with the glory I had with you before the world began' (John 17:5). That's it! All things were made, said Paul. In Him, God made the world in wisdom. But the Son of God is the Wisdom of God. Therefore, God made the world in Christ.

We are not here just talking about the divine mind. We are talking about One who became incarnate and walked this earth among us. All things were created in Him. And then– to add to it–all things were created by Him, through Him, by means of Him. If you want the technical term, the Son was the Father's agent, acting on the Father's behalf in the creation of the world; and, of course, in much more. In fact, if you want a nice study to follow through the New Testament, you will discover that again and again, when the Father wants to deal with the world, He deals through the Son. The Son is not only the agent of creation. He is the agent of providence, He upholds the world by the powerful Word.

All things hold together in Him. He is the agent of revelation. In Him was life and the life was the light of men. He's the agent of redemption. That's a truism, we all know that, don't we? God saved us through His Son. God will judge the world one day by that man He has appointed. That man is of course, His own incarnate Son, Jesus Christ, and here He is the agent of creation, the One through whom the Father made the world. 'I was the craftsman at His side'–Jesus fulfils that old poetry in ways that its writer could never have understood.

You could put placards on the mountains and the seashore, the rivers and the hills: 'Jesus the Son of God, designer and constructor'.

All things were created in Him and by Him–and thirdly, for Him. Why did the world come into existence in the first place? Why was everything made? It was made for the Son, for His possession, dominion, inheritance. That is what Paul is saying here. It's all His–including you and me. After all, we are included in 'all things', aren't we? And in a very special way, for we were made in God's image (note the subtle difference: He is the image, we are made in the image). Certainly we were created in Christ just like the rest. We are part of the 'all things'.

That's why coming to know the Lord Jesus Christ and yielding to Him is to do the most natural thing in the world, supernaturally; because you were made for Him in the first place.

Now, go back to Colossians 1. That's what the little word 'firstborn' means. The firstborn of all creation–or 'over all creation' as the NIV translates it–doesn't mean 'the first creature to come into existence'. The firstborn was the heir. Paul is saying, 'It's all His, everything is His, all things are His, for all things were created, in Him, by Him, for Him. He is the firstborn of creation.'

Do you know, the rabbis even used that phrase about God. They called Him the firstborn of creation. For New Testament authors like Paul it's the Son. He is the firstborn and therefore as it is all His, He is rightful Lord over all and was so long before He came into this world to win it back from Satan's insolent bondage. It was all His before a shot was fired. The creation writes about the Son Of God.

Now, those are the facts. Just think of the implications. What a staggering thought this is! You see, Paul is talking about a real person. Not a mythological person but a historical person, a man who had been contemporary. Someone who had walked this earth, who had eaten and slept and spoken and lived among them. He is saying, 'This is the Wisdom of God.'

And it accords with so many other statements made by the Apostle and others in the New Testament about Jesus. Do you notice how they lift Old Testament references to the Lord God Almighty and give them without apology to the Lord Jesus Christ?

When Philippians 2:10-11 speaks about every knee bowing, every tongue confessing, it is an allusion to a passage in Isaiah that originally referred to the Lord God Almighty. Look at all the ways in which Paul here describes the Son of God: He is the very nature of God, the form of God, the image of God, the glory of God; in Christ the whole fullness of the Deity lives in bodily form (2:9).

Now, let's remember who is writing this. This man was reared as a Jew, reared to say with his dying breath, 'Hear O Israel, the Lord our God is one.' He is speaking about the Son in divine terms: all things were created in Him, and by Him, and for Him. And all I can say is, something massive must have happened to Paul and to the others to turn their thinking upside down and inside out. And of course in Paul's case we know what it was. He met the glorified Lord. Read through his letters: it colours everything he writes about Jesus thereafter. It was a tremendous encouragement to him.

He began to realise that this Jesus whom he was persecuting was not just a heretical carpenter from a despised Galilean village, He was Lord of all. Not only by redemption right but by creation right. He was the firstborn of all creation. A staggering thing! I never cease to be amazed at how the New Testament authors speak of Jesus.

Secondly, it was a tremendous encouragement to those to whom He wrote. Let us stress the spiritual side of creation here. 'All things visible and invisible'—he goes on to list the principalities and powers, the authorities. Not just political powers, oh no! Reading between the lines in this letter, we know that the church at Colosse was vexed by false teachers who said, 'Well, it's very nice to believe in the Lord Jesus Christ, but you've got to take on board these spiritual beings as well, these rulers, authorities—angels, demons, call them what you will.'

Now you can see how Paul tries to undercut that teaching. Today we either ignore the supernatural creation altogether, or we become obsessed with it. Paul is implying here, 'You must be aware of the spiritual implication; all these things were created, yes, but let's put them in their proper perspective; they were all created in Christ, by Christ and for Christ. The Christ you own and trust is the firstborn, and therefore you have nothing to fear from the spiritual creation. He is all you need.'

Then thirdly, there is a tremendous encouragement for us too. As we said: if the Son is the firstborn, He is the heir. In Romans 8:17 Paul described Christians as co-heirs with Christ. And there is a sense in which that happens here and now. When you become a Christian you begin to see the world with different eyes.

D. L. Moody recorded that on the day he was converted in Boston, 'The old sun seemed to shine the brighter, the birds seemed to sing the sweeter. I fell in love with the birds that day.' Now that's rather different from the somewhat pathetic attempts that are being made to give ecology a spiritual direction; people start personifying nature, there's a resurgence of pantheism and nature religion and the belief that all things are God. It is New Age teaching.

But go to the Bible: God and His creation are separate. The creator stands over against His creation. He brings it into being, in and by and for His Son. And it is only when you come to terms with His Son that you begin to realise its true significance.

And what of the future?

More than once in the New Testament, redemption is described in terms of re-creation. The Son, we are told, will sum up all things in Himself. He reconciles all things to

Himself. There'll be a new heaven and a new earth in which righteousness dwells. If this world with all its beauty and awesome splendour is a fallen world under the curse of man's sin—a world, according to Paul, 'groaning in travail until set free from its bondage to decay', what will the new heaven and earth be like? Created in true righteousness, no less.

We make heaven pretty insubstantial. No wonder people don't want to go there. For, you see, the One in and through and for whom it was all made came into this world, verse 20, 'to reconcile to himself all things, whether things on earth or things in heaven, by making peace through his blood, shed on the cross'. That is even more staggering!

> Come, see His hands and His feet,
> the scars that speak of sacrifice,
> hands that flung stars into space,
> to cruel nails surrendered.
>
> Graham Kendrick

The crucifixion of Jesus was not merely the martyrdom of a good man. It was, incredibly, the heir of the universe, the firstborn of all creation, dying in the form of one of His creatures, to win back what was already His by creation right. Doesn't that want to make you stop and wonder and worship?

KNOWING THE WAY BACK

by Rev. David Coffey

Psalm 51

If the forgiveness of a human being is sweet, how much more the forgiveness of the living God!

This morning Dr Kendall told us that most Christians feel guilty about something. And I believe you can have false guilt, about which we need to be assured we do not have to worry, and you can have true guilt, where sin is unconfessed because it has not been identified as sin. And of that sin, we need to be forgiven.

I was reading recently about something that has become all too common in modern life. It was a tale of sexual passion that led to adultery. The wife's lover arranged for her husband to be murdered. This was not a story in my daily newspaper, but is told in 2 Samuel 11 and 12. The names of the lovers were David and Bathsheba; the murdered husband was the army commander, Uriah.

The Bible says that what David did displeased the Lord, and it took Nathan as God's messenger to bring him to his senses. And David sought to do what everybody who's been in that situation seeks to do; he sought to untangle the social and personal consequences of his sin.

What you have before you in Psalm 51 is the 'knowing the way back' psalm. It's not just for murderers and adulterers, though it's certainly for them; it's for all people who seek the peace and presence of God which they have lost. Thousands and thousands of sinners–many here this evening–have found their way back, long after they had given up hope, through the words of this psalm.

May I issue a spiritual health warning? Do not fear God's open-heart surgery when you come to a passage like this. You know the old Puritan saying, 'Grace is to buried sin what water is to fire'. God wants to bring His grace out of these verses this evening to deal with that sin. As water to fire, so His grace to our sin.

Know that you belong (verses 1–2)

When you are seeking the way back, the first thing is to know that you belong. For all his wretchedness, David knows he still belongs to God. He appeals to His mercy and grace (verse 1). He's an undeserving candidate for undeserved grace. He appeals to the loyal love, the unfailing love of God who has made a covenant commitment between Himself and His people. David's part in it has been broken. He's depending upon God's loyal, covenant love. He appeals to the compassion of God. The word used here in verse 1 is associated with the feelings a mother has for her children. Just think of the compassion that Jesus had for people during His earthly ministry!–and that compassion is abroad this evening.

David begins his appeal by knowing that he belongs. That's where you must begin, because if you do you can then direct your heart-needs to God. You can see in verses 1 and 2 that David has three heart-needs. The first, 'blot out my transgression'–in other words, 'I have a record that needs to be cleared.' The second, 'Wash away all my iniquity'–in other words, 'I have the need to be thoroughly scrubbed clean; a gentle rinse will not do, so deep has this gone.' And the third, 'Cleanse me ...'—in other words, 'I'm an outcast who needs to be received back.'

These are the words of somebody who no longer feels at home in the company of God's people, an outcast from fellowship and worship. So these are his *needs*, not his *feelings*. They describe his actual standing before God. Begin by knowing that you belong, and then you will have the encouragement to bring those heartfelt needs which describe your condition.

A couple of years ago I took part with others in one of those Sunday morning live television services on television, in which I said 'Jesus is not shocked by sin, He's drawn towards it.' By two o'clock I had received one note through the door and one telephone call from somebody living at least 200 miles away, asking 'Is it true what you say?' On the Monday morning I walked down the street and a traffic warden told me he had watched the programme. He had picked up those words. But the most amazing of all was to go to a local shop where I knew the manager. He had watched the service too. And he broke down in tears, and said 'Why am I crying? And why did I cry yesterday?' I'm not going to tell you his story, but that conversation in the shop led to a meeting in his home, and it was all to do with those words, 'Jesus is not shocked by sin, but drawn to it.'

That is what the cross is all about! And you begin by knowing that you belong. It's a daring thought, but it's on those grounds alone that God can address you in your need, and in your need you can address God: 'Have mercy on me, O God, according to Your loyal love; and according to Your great compassion.'

Recognise sin for what it is (verses 3–6)

You need to have the courage to deal with that sin which you know you carry in your life, unconfessed and un-acknowledged as sin. That lies at the heart of all true confession. That's what David says in verse 3: 'I know my sin'—it has the idea of 'I'm constantly aware of my sin, my sin is always before me, I am face-to-face with it.'

He goes on to recognise sin for what it is, using specific words. In verse 1, 'Blot out my transgressions' has the idea of a revolt, of self-assertion: 'Blot out my rebellion'. It's incredible for New Testament Christians like you and me to look at our sin in such terms. Surely the cross dealt with me as a rebel? And yet I am still capable of rebelling.

And we look at this word again in verse 2: 'Wash away my iniquity'—my waywardness. Someone who loves to wander is a wayward person, deliberately choosing the wrong road. That's the meaning of 'iniquity' or 'waywardness'.

And the third word David uses, at the end of verse 2, is

'sin'—my failure, my own deliberate fault which I cannot blame on anybody else.

So whether it be my rebellion or waywardness or my failure, I have deliberately veered off the road that God wants me to travel. I have before me the map of God's righteous plan for living and I have chosen to put the map on one side and walk my own way. That's what this psalm is saying—remember, from somebody who is seeking the way back.

In verse 4 we read that this rebellion, waywardness and failure in the eyes of the then known world, was really David's sin against God. David says, 'I've done this against you Lord.' And is not this what he is saying in verse 4—'Lord, when Nathan came in and spoke Your word, "You are the man", I agreed with Your verdict.'?

'You are proved right when you speak'—'And, Lord, You are justified when You judge. Lord, in the Keswick Convention tent in July 1991, when You come and say "You are the man", and "You are the woman", Lord I want to say that I agree with the verdict. You are right when You speak, and You are justified when you judge.' That's recognising sin for what it is.

David goes on (verse 5) to say, 'I was... sinful from the time my mother conceived me.' He isn't talking about the process of human procreation. He goes to the very roots of his existence, saying 'Sin has pervaded my existence from the beginning.'

In verse 6, what David is really saying is: 'The exact opposite of what God requires has happened in my life.' Some indeed link verses 5 and 6. We were hearing something of that in this morning's Bible Reading—the prophecy concerning the twins in the womb, God teaching truth in the inner parts and wisdom in the inmost place. But however you interpret the verse, David is saying 'I am not the way God intended me to be. There is no truth in me.'

Ask God to apply His cure (verses 7–9)

Thirdly, having understood that you belong and recognised sin for what it is, you then ask God to apply His cure. You can see the words in these verses: 'cleanse me', 'wash me', 'let me hear joy and gladness', 'hide your face from my sins' (there's that word again), 'blot out all my iniquity'.

This is asking God to apply His cure. Verse 7: 'Lord, cleanse me. I want the cure for the leper and the outcast.' The cure in both David's day and Jesus' when He healed the ten lepers was a branch of hyssop dipped in sacrificial blood and applied to the person concerned—but then the pronouncement, 'You are clean'. David picks that up: 'Cleanse me in the method that has been laid down in Your word, with hyssop; and let me hear the announcement "You are clean".'

Not according to the sacrificial laws laid down for David and his generation, but, for this people, that Other blood-sacrifice which you know well about, and the pronouncement that Jesus alone can give: 'You are declared clean according to your faith, let it be.' Apply to God for His cure: 'Wash me' (verse 7). David is saying, 'I apply for the cure of a deeply stained life'. Remember, not a gentle rinse but a thorough scrub.

Jeremiah talks about people finding that soap and detergent will not touch the stain that is in them. But 'if we confess our sins, he is faithful and just'—according to His loyal love—'and will purify us from all unrighteousness' (1 John 1:9).

In verse 8, asking God to apply his cure, he says 'Speak to me.' David does not now want to hear 'Thou art the man'. That was the word that brought him to his senses, but he now wants to hear joy and gladness from that same God, and he wants dancing bones, 'Let the bones you have crushed rejoice.'

So what's the cure for the one who wants to return home and hear those words? That was the Prodigal's problem. He wanted to come home but he wasn't sure what word he would hear. And what was the word? 'Let's rejoice, because this my child that was lost is found, and this my son that was dead is alive' (see Luke 15:11–32).

And God wants to apply the cure (verse 8): 'Cleanse me, wash me, speak to me, and clear me. Hide your face from my sins and blot out my record.'

This is asking for the debtor's cure. 'Lord, turn your face back towards me and tell me what I need to hear: "So far as the East is from the West—infinity!—so far have I removed your sin from you." '

Dear friend, wherever you are this evening, I ask you to come and stand under the shadow of Calvary itself. And as you stand there, and understand afresh all that the Saviour has done for you, will you receive afresh God's cure for sin? Grace is to sin what water is to fire.

Ask God to perform His miracle (verses 10–12)

That word 'create' in verse 10 is only ever used in connection with God's work. This is something that a human being can never do for themselves.

In every house I've lived in I've been grateful that there has been a rubbish dump nearby. I have had some fairly low-class dumps near where I've lived, but now we've moved to Oxfordshire we have the most high-class dump that I've ever had near to my house. You would be pleased to take your grandmother there for tea! It's swept clean, it's a beautiful place. But I tell you, whatever the class of dump, there's a tremendous feeling of relief when you've emptied the rubbish there and you drive away with an empty car boot.

Recently I've been removing rubbish from our garage so that I can create a study in it and line the walls with books. I've taken quantities of rubbish to the dump. Do you realise, that when we move into verse 10, with that word 'create', we're not just talking negatively about dealing with sin, about knowing the way back; we've now moved into doing something with that empty room of yours that has been cleansed and cleaned?

I want us to go much farther than the psalmist David could ever go. As we move into the Everest of Romans chapter 8, out of the 'wretched man' passage of chapter 7, 'Praise God,' says Paul: 'Thanks be to God according to the Lord Jesus Christ, the work of creating the new heart in the believer has happened!'

'If the Spirit of him who raised Jesus from the dead is living in you, he who raised Christ from the dead will also give life to your mortal bodies through his Spirit, who lives in you' (Rom. 8:11).

Read those verses 10 to 12 as a New Testament Christian.

Add to them in a way that David could never add to them, and recognise what I believe these verses are saying when they use the phrases, 'renew a steadfast spirit...take not your Holy Spirit...and grant me a willing spirit'. Recognise that it is talking of this activity of the Holy Spirit who has been shed abroad in our hearts. That is the creation of the clean and the pure heart. Praise God, it's happened! It's begun here on earth to be completed in heaven.

Anticipate a future ministry (verses 13–19)

Verse 13: there will be teaching, very specific teaching, teaching the wayward the way. And what better person to do it than you?

Secondly, there will be testimony. Brothers and sisters, what this verse is saying is this: there is blood on our hands here as teachers of the word, if we do not apply the teaching of Psalm 51. You may say, why such a message this evening to such a gathering as this? There will be blood on our hands if we don't warn you about the dangers of flirting in the way that David and Bathsheba flirted. You say, that's incredible: to think that in a conference like this, this might be relevant. But if God says it's relevant to your life then it is relevant. I would dare to say that someone here this evening may need to make a telephone call and go home. There is blood on our hands if we don't bear testimony to these things, especially concerning the way back.

And, verse 15, there will be praise. As somebody has said, your car may take you to church, but it needs God to open your mouth when you get there. 'Open my lips, because up till now Lord, carrying this guilt, the words that I sing mocked me–but no more.' The mark of a new man or woman in Christ, the creation of the new heart, is that God can open your lips in praise and thanksgiving.

Verses 16–18, there will be meaningful worship: not a rejection of sacrifice, but the best gifts are accompanied by a crushed heart.

And in verses 18 and 19, there will be corporate blessings. Notice how it begins with personal repentance and leads to the prosperity of a whole city. Some of you will know how sin can spoil a family, a church and a nation; well, surely the opposite is true. Repentance and forgiveness can bless a family, a church and a nation.

As we close, look at verse 8 again: dancing bones–'Let the bones you have crushed rejoice.' I was privileged a couple of years ago to take a missionary retreat in Africa. On the Sunday morning we gathered for a communion service. They were a group of pretty ordinary Christians. They had their problems. There were tensions and strains which had not really emerged for God's healing at the retreat thus far. As we sat around the Lord's table, for a little while we just sat in silence; and then, through the open windows, came the sound of singing from the French-speaking congregation of the International Church.

My French is not very good but I recognised the tune and I know the English words.

> There is power, power, wonder-working power
> In the precious blood of the Lamb...

We came to the moment for the Peace, which as you can imagine was very relevant in that particular situation. It went on for several minutes. The joy, the tears of repentance, the reconciliation!

Can I hold out to you the promise of dancing bones? Do you know the way back? Do you know 'There's a way back to God from the dark paths of sin, there's a door that is open and you–you–may go in. At Calvary's cross–as a sinner–you begin, when you come as that sinner to Jesus'.

Let's sing it as a prayer blessing to those in this tent this evening who need to know there is a way back.

THE GIFT THE FATHER PROMISED

by Rev. David Jackman

Acts 1:1–8

For centuries the Jewish nation had been waiting for the Messiah to appear. He would restore the kingdom to Israel. Down through the centuries of the prophetic ministry they had been taught that great David's greater son would extend the rule of the Lord far beyond the bounds of David's geographical kingdom. Not only would it be a great expansion of the whole earthly kingdom of Israel, but it would bring in a new dimension of spiritual life and vitality.

Listen, for example, to the prophet Ezekiel, writing in chapter 37: 'I will put my Spirit in you and you will live, and I will settle you in your own land ... They will live in the land I gave to my servant Jacob, the land where your fathers lived ... I will make a covenant of peace with them ... and I will put my sanctuary among them for ever. My dwelling-place will be with them; I will be their God, and they will be my people' (Ezek. 37:14, 25–27).

But the return of the exiles from Babylon had fulfilled that glorious promise only very partially. And they waited down the centuries for the gift of the Messiah. Then He came: 'The Word was made flesh and tabernacled for a while amongst us.' And gradually a group, mainly Galileans, came to see that the only explanation of this amazing Person with whom they were living was that He was the Christ, the Son of God.

It was a slow road to understanding. The way to faith is always the way of understanding, through the mind to the will; it took them time to get there. But almost as soon as they recognised who He was and said 'You are the Christ, the Son of the living God', He began to talk about leaving them, about going to Jerusalem to suffer and to die.

When it all happened, and they saw Him hung up on that cross, it was as though their whole world had shattered. The gift had been taken away. 'We trusted that he was the One who was going to redeem Israel' (Luke 24:21).

And though in the wonder of the resurrection He was restored to them, it wasn't the same. Do you remember how He said to Mary in the garden, 'Do not hold on to me, for I have not yet returned to the Father' (John 20:17)? And Luke, in volume one of his work, the great Gospel of Luke, tells us that when Jesus began to go up to Jerusalem He resolutely set His face to go because the time approached for Him to be taken up to heaven (see Luke 9:51). As far as Luke was concerned the Jerusalem journey, which takes up such a large part of his Gospel, is not just a journey to the cross and the resurrection, but primarily a journey back to heaven through the cross and resurrection.

And what happens when the gift has gone, when the earthly tent of Jesus has disappeared? Is that the end of it? Do these disciples just have lovely memories to look back on, an inspiring story to encourage them to try to live up to what Jesus taught? Is that all Christianity has to offer?

You know, there are millions of people who think so, and thousands of Christians who live as if it were so. They see Jesus as having set the agenda for us and given us a great example, and believe that now we must call on God 'up there' to help us 'down here' when we get stuck. 'Heaven helps those who help themselves.'

It couldn't be further from the truth. The gift that the Father promised means that heaven helps those who cannot help themselves. The help is the gift of the person of God the Holy Spirit.

I want us to think about three aspects of this great gift of the Father. Firstly, let's look at

The Spirit's activity

The forty days between the resurrection and the ascension of Jesus were a transition period. If we haven't understood the truth of the Bible, then we shall never get it right in our experience. So we need to understand what Jesus is here teaching His disciples about the Spirit's activity; for in these forty days He begins to demonstrate to them the new post-resurrection order.

During those days, verse 3 tells us, He gave many convincing proofs that He was alive, and He spoke about the kingdom. A similar phrase in the preceding verse, verse 2, is that He gave instructions, through the Holy Spirit, to the apostles. So Jesus is doing two things: He is doing something and teaching something. He is proving His resurrected glory, demonstrating it beyond any doubt, and He is teaching them truth through the Holy Spirit about the kingdom of God. The end of the earthly stage of Christ's ministry has arrived. This is the beginning of something new.

Luke is beginning his second volume, dedicated, like his Gospel, to Theophilus. He says that he has already carefully researched a reliable account of the beginnings of Christianity. Here in volume two he states this underlying principle by which all that follows must be interpreted: 'All that Jesus began to do and to teach until the day He was taken up to heaven.' Right at the start, Luke is telling us that the earthly ministry of Jesus, including the cross and the Resurrection, was in a sense only the beginning.

Of course it was a completed work. Of course He did everything that was necessary for our salvation. We are right to speak about 'the finished work of Christ'. But He now continues to work in the world through His people, the body of Christ; animated by His risen life, every Christian a part.

At the outset Luke is indicating that the teaching ministry of Jesus was carried out through the Holy Spirit. That's how He gave instructions to His apostles. Jesus Himself says in Matthew 12:28 'I drive out demons by the Spirit of God.' In the synagogue, at the beginning of His ministry, He said 'The Spirit of the Lord is on me, because he has anointed me to preach good news to the poor' (Luke 4:18). His miracles, teaching, actions and words were always through the power of the Holy Spirit, and indeed the writer to the Hebrews tells us that this was true of His redemptive work as well: 'The blood of Christ, who through the eternal Spirit offered himself unblemished to God, [will] cleanse our consciences from acts that lead to death, so that we may serve the living God!' (Heb 9:14).

This is the Spirit's activity. The whole earthly ministry of our Lord Jesus Christ as man depended upon the Holy Spirit in every aspect. If that is true, then how much more does His body on earth, the church, need that same enabling of the Holy Spirit in order to function properly in the world today! One of the words used for the Spirit is *parakletos*—'Comforter'. In English it means 'the one who is called alongside to help'. And as the Holy Spirit instructs us in the word of scripture, protects us, strengthens and enables us, so the whole work of the Lord Jesus in the world moves forward by the activity of the Spirit in the hearts and minds and lives of His people.

He is not given an independent work or existence, for the Holy Spirit *is* Jesus, at work in the continuation of His ministry. He said to His disciples just before His death, 'I will not leave you as orphans. I will send to you another comforter' (see John 14). And you may know that the adjective 'another' means 'one exactly the same'. The word means that the Holy Spirit is not a substitute for Jesus, but because He too is 'in His very nature God', He is another comforter of exactly the same sort.

So the deity of the Holy Spirit is firmly established by the Lord Jesus. And we are to understand that the acts of the Holy Spirit through the apostles are the extension of the ministry begun by the Lord Jesus and now continued through His Spirit. That says to us that the church, and the individual ministries of Christians like us, will never make progress unless they are energized by the ministry of the Holy Spirit.

It's true in evangelism—it's the Holy Spirit who takes the things of Christ and makes them real and living. It's true when we come to faith—it's He who opens our eyes to see who the Lord Jesus is. It's the Holy Spirit who convicts us of sin, righteousness and judgement. It's the Holy Spirit who brings us to the new birth, who indwells the believer—to make us more and more into the image of Christ. All on the grounds of what Christ has done on Calvary; but it is the Spirit's activity, to make us the people of God.

So the Lord Jesus is teaching the disciples how vital that ministry is going to be. And every time we try to do Christian work without depending on God's Spirit to give us wisdom, thinking 'I've done this so often I can do it today too', we are denying the very foundation of the gospel and the church. 'Without Me' said Jesus, 'You can do nothing.' But He's left His Spirit till the work on earth is done.

The Spirit's availability

Look with me at verse 5. Our Lord Jesus says to the disciples 'In a few days you will be baptised with the Holy Spirit.' That, of course, was promised at the very beginning of His ministry, and in all of the four Gospels John the Baptist is recorded as pointing to Jesus as the One who will baptise not with water, but with the Holy Spirit and with fire. John says that this was revealed to Him by God as he saw the Spirit come down and remain on Jesus at the time of His baptism in the water.

Notice, that promise is a passive promise. It is something Jesus says will happen to you, not by your own efforts but because He, the Sovereign Lord, promises it as an expression of His will. Luke expresses it differently at the end of his Gospel (volume one), when he quotes Jesus' words: 'I am going to send you what my Father has promised; but stay in the city until you have been clothed with power from on high' (Luke 24:29).

Now, what he's saying in both references is that the Holy Spirit is not a human achievement but a divine gift; that He is utterly out of our reach unless God the Father sends the Spirit. They had to stay in Jerusalem and wait. It was a geographical condition for them. Actually in the original it's the word 'Jerusalem' that is emphatic, not the word 'waiting'. Jesus commanded them to do that because Pentecost was imminent, and it had to occur in the Holy City in fulfilment of all the promises. And He wanted His people to be all together, in that place, on that day.

That doesn't mean we should infer from that where we

should wait, or indeed that we need to wait for the Spirit. They didn't secure the Holy Spirit as they waited in prayer; He came as the gift of the Father. That is the difference between being an Old Testament and a New Testament believer. We believe, don't we, that the two Testaments are one book. But there are differences, of course.

To understand that more fully, turn back to John 7 and those lovely words of Jesus–'On the last and greatest day of the Feast, Jesus stood and said in a loud voice, "If anyone is thirsty, let him come to me and drink. Whoever believes in me, as the Scripture has said, rivers of living water will flow from within him." By this He meant the Spirit, whom those who believed in Him were later to receive. Up to that time the Spirit had not been given, since Jesus had not yet been glorified' (John 7:37–38).

Now of course the Holy Spirit was active. From the beginning of Genesis 1 He brooded on the waters and was the agent of Creation; but, although the Spirit was always God and is therefore eternally God, the Spirit was not yet given– not in the sense in which He is given to these disciples following the glorification of Jesus.

In the Old Testament, the Spirit came upon people and left them. He 'clothed Himself' with Gideon. He 'came upon' King David. At times He came upon men who were being called to do particular work in the tabernacle; the craftsmen were 'empowered by the Spirit'. But they didn't know the Spirit indwelling them in the way in which New Testament believers do. The Spirit was not yet given in that way, because Jesus had not yet died on the cross and been raised again. It is the 'fruit of the glorification of Jesus', which in John's Gospel means His lifting up on the cross, that enables the Father to send the Spirit into the lives of the redeemed community.

And that is why the gift of the Spirit is such a revolutionary dynamic. It is the Father's gift. It is not a responsibility, it is not an opportunity; it is not even a privilege to be claimed. It is the promise of a free gift of God that Jesus gives to these apostles. And wherever that 'promise' word is used in the New Testament, it is always contrasted with human effort.

Turn back with me to Acts 2:38, where at the end of the

day of Pentecost Peter is coming to the close of that great sermon. You'll find the same thing there: 'And you will receive the gift of the Holy Spirit. The promise is for you and your children and for all who are far off–for all whom the Lord our God will call.' So it's not just to the apostles, it is to every Christian down through the generations, to all who are called by the gospel into relationship with God, that the free gift of the Holy Spirit is promised by the Father. And the baptism that Jesus talks about, which they received on the day of Pentecost, is receiving the Holy Spirit personally.

We call that day the birthday of the church. Ever since, whenever men and women have repented and believed the good news, the Holy Spirit has come to take up residence within their personalities. We have been baptised in the Spirit when we turn from our sin and trust the Lord Jesus Christ as our Saviour and King.

This is the gift the Father gives to every one of His people. So in every passage in Acts where people become Christians, they receive the Holy Spirit. The two things are the same. The Holy Spirit is always called either the 'promise' or the 'gift'; never obtained by human effort, but always the gift of God's grace.

There is no 'maybe' in Acts 1:5. 'You will be,' He says, 'baptised with the Holy Spirit.' He doesn't say 'if you fulfil certain conditions' but, 'all of you will be'. And if you look again at 2:1–4–the account of Pentecost–you'll see how the emphasis is upon the comprehensive nature of it. 'They saw what seemed to be tongues of fire that separated and came to rest on the most holy ones among them'–it doesn't say that, does it? No; 'each of them'. Some of them? No. All of them were filled with the Holy Spirit.

So you see it is a promise for everyone whom He calls. It is the promise that was fulfilled on the day of Pentecost as 3,000 were added to the church and baptised–and they too received the gift that the Father sent. It is an overflowing gift of God's grace. And the lovely thing is this: He does not send His gifts; He is the gift. If you're a Christian tonight, the glorious truth at the heart of this passage is that the Holy Spirit is available to you now, because He dwells within you if you've turned in faith to the Lord Jesus Christ.

Sometimes we talk loosely about receiving more of the Spirit. But the Holy Spirit is a person, you can't receive Him in instalments. To every believer He is God's free gift. And there is no implication, in the Acts of the Apostles, that a subjective measure of faith or depth of obedience are necessary. He is the Father's promised gift that everyone who turns to Christ experiences for themselves.

Of course, I'm not saying that we don't need to be refilled with the Spirit, to be constantly, as Paul says to the Ephesians, 'being filled'; that our lives need to be open each day to the life of God to flow within us, and that that life needs to spread into every area of our experience and personality. But being filled with the Spirit is not getting more of the Spirit: it is the Spirit penetrating the different areas of our lives in which we have held out against His sovereign rule and His loving and convicting grace.

And as I open up each different door to Him and God shows me different areas of my life on which He wants to put His finger; and when I respond 'Lord, I can't do it, but You can. You've given me the gift of Your Spirit within me. So Lord Jesus, take control, and fill me in this area, and in every area of my life'–then the gift of God flows in His fullness.

And I find, as I'm sure you do, that when I do open up an area of my life to God afresh, then within twenty-four hours He shows me another one. We need constantly to be 'being' filled with the Holy Spirit, the gift that the Father has promised.

So, you see, this is not a difficult doctrine. There's no magic formula by which we might persuade God to be gracious and give His Spirit to us. He is available to everyone. None of us has less of the Holy Spirit than we really want. We quench the Spirit, we grieve the Spirit, we exclude Him from certain areas of our lives. And often at events like Keswick, and sometimes in the quietness of our own hearts, God just touches our lives and says, 'That's what I want to change.'

When you yield to the ministry of the Holy Spirit in that way, there comes fresh awareness of His love and grace and power. So every Christian finds that the promise is fulfilled whenever we turn to the Lord. We are deeply cleansed by the blood of Jesus. We are immersed (which is the idea of baptism, meaning basically 'soaking'), we are soaked in the Spirit. There is a new environment in which we now live.

Baptism of course is a picture of initiation. That's why it comes right at the beginning of Christian experience. And it is the baptism in the Spirit, which we call by various titles, that is our initiation into the very life of God. So that, as Paul says, 'No longer are we controlled by the sinful nature, but by the Spirit of God in you, and if anyone doesn't have the Spirit of Christ, he doesn't belong to Christ' (see Rom. 8:9). But the corollary of that is that if you belong to Christ you have the Spirit. He is available. You've been made alive–by Him.

The Spirit's agenda

I have always been encouraged by the disciples, because it seems to take as long for the penny to drop for them as for me in many situations of life. And even at this late stage the apostles are still getting it wrong–for example in verse 6, where they are once again on the wrong track, there's still this lingering hope in their minds of an earthly kingdom.

They're still thinking contrary to the concerns of the Lord. His agenda is very different; He is not interested in earthly-style lordship or the restoration of political power to Israel. But He is interested in a world-wide spread of the kingly rule of Christ. That is His great concern: that this gospel should be preached to all the nations.

So the Father's gift is a dynamic to get a task completed. Acts 1:8 says 'You will receive power.' It's that famous word *dunamis*, which at root means 'the ability to get the job done.' That's what we need, isn't it? The ability to complete the task. The universal declaration of the gospel of Jesus Christ is the task. The ability to get the task done, verse 8 says, is the Holy Spirit coming upon you.

Now notice again that the symbolism 'from above' teaches us again that He is the gift of the Father. That means that the gift is independent of my emotional state. I don't have to 'feel right' in order to receive and experience the power of the Holy Spirit. And it is independent of my spiritual attainment. Because we're so works-religion oriented, we tend to feel that unless our spiritual lives are up to a certain level we cannot possibly expect the Holy Spirit to use us. Don't you sometimes feel like that? You look back over your life this last week, or at a period in your life, and you say 'Well, really, it's C-minus, or even D-plus this week, so God couldn't possibly use me.' And a few C-minus's like that and you soon get completely demoralised and discouraged.

But, you see, the gift of the Spirit is nothing to do with your spiritual attainment. He comes from above, upon us; He comes from outside, within us. 'And when God comes upon His people there is ability to get the job done.'

The power that so many people are interested in today is not power for it's own sake, much less power for our sakes; it is the power for God's purposes to be fulfilled in other's lives. That's why He's given His Spirit. In Luke 24 Jesus says to the disciples, 'You are witnesses of these things, that is, My death and resurrection; that's an objective fact, you're the witnesses, you saw it happen.' Here, in Acts 1, He says 'You shall be my witnesses. Not just that you are objectively the witnesses because you're there, but you will personally be involved in witnessing.'

Jesus is saying 'You've got an objective witness, you apostles, because you've seen Me die and rise again, but I am going to send My Spirit to make that objective fact into a personal experience.' And the power, by word and by life, to bear testimony to the reality of the fact that Jesus Christ is Lord, is the power of the Holy Spirit.

F. D. Brunner puts it like this: 'The power of the Holy Spirit is the ability to join men and women to the risen Christ so that they are able to represent Him;—I like that—'there is no higher blessing.'

'You will receive power and you will be My witnesses.' The primary reference is to the apostles, and we are the fruit of their witness. Why do we believe that Jesus died and rose again? Because the apostles, who saw it, wrote it down in scripture, and because by the Holy Spirit's ministry our minds and wills have been opened to that truth. We are not witnesses in the sense in which they were. They are the witnesses, and if their witness is insufficient then we remain rebellious and ignorant. That's why our task is not so much to communicate *our* testimony, as to communicate the apostolic testimony.

For the Spirit's agenda is not first that we tell people about our experience, but that we tell people about the truth concerning the Lord Jesus; and that that message of truth, as verse 8 says, should be taken 'to the ends of the earth'. Of course we support that in a sense, by saying 'And I have found it to be true in my experience.' And Christian testimony, personal testimony, has a valuable part to play. But the heart of the gospel is not my experience; it is Christ and His work.

And the Spirit is concerned to spread the knowledge of the Lord Jesus–everywhere.

Now this could not be more clearly seen than when the gift is given at Pentecost. Let me just point it out to you very quickly from chapter 2. What happened when the Spirit came? They began to speak in other tongues or languages, as the Spirit enabled them. The people who were in Jerusalem from all over the world said 'We hear them declaring the wonders of God in our own tongues' (2:11). God enabled them, miraculously, to speak in languages that these people knew and could understand. Why? Because He wanted, through the gift of the Spirit, to communicate the wonders of God–truth–in words.

What is Peter's explanation of this, when he starts to preach? He quotes from Joel: 'This is the fulfilment of that prophecy that "Even on my servants, both men and women, I will pour out my Spirit in those days, and they will prophesy" ' (see verse 18). Whatever your definition of prophecy, I think all Christians are agreed that it has in its heart the idea of speaking forth the word of God. So when the Spirit comes in power, what is His mark in the lives of God's people, both men and women, all His servants? It is that they speak forth His word. That's why the Spirit is given, in order that the truth of God's word may be communicated. That's the Spirit's agenda.

And what is the purpose of that gift, of the word of God to the world through His church? 'Everyone who calls on the name of the Lord will be saved.' So why has the Spirit come? In order that people from all over the world may hear the wonderful deeds of God, that they may hear the word of God spoken to them in ways they understand so that they will be saved. That's why the Spirit is sent: for world evangelisation.

And that's what Peter does. He continues his sermon (verse 22) talking about Jesus. He was a man, but 'a man accredited by God to you by miracles, wonders and signs.' He talks in verse 23 about His death upon the cross. He proclaims in verse 24 His resurrection from the dead. He says in verse 32 that they are the 'witnesses of the fact'; it's got historical foundations. 'We don't believe a gospel that's made up out of wishful stories, it happened in history.' And on the basis of what happened in history we are saved, through the objective work of Christ on the cross on our behalf.

His unique position is described in verse 32, 'We're a witness of these things.' But he exemplifies how the Spirit will work in the future by calling them, in verse 36, to acknowledge that 'God has made this Jesus, whom you crucified, both Lord and Christ.' And then he calls them to repent, to believe...and the gift goes on–'You will receive the gift of the Holy Spirit.' You say 'But I'm not a preacher and I can't be involved in that.' Listen, the Holy Spirit has the ability to enable you to speak for Jesus. Not just by the words that you speak but by the life that you live.

Both go together, you see. Some of us who are not so good at the speaking say 'Ah yes, I'll join the silent service.' Well, of course your holy life counts for Jesus. It's the Holy Spirit who enables you to live more like the Lord Jesus, and who reveals Christ through you. And it's no good opening your mouth if your life doesn't support it. Because what you are shouts so loud, people won't hear what you say. But He wants our lives and our lips, together, to be in His service.

The holiness of life that we've been called to this week, my friends, is not a warm feeling at the end of a meeting, nor the ability to live the life-style of the cultural sub-group of Christians to which we happen to belong. Holiness of life is being like Jesus. Christlikeness is having a heart for lost people, beating in tune with Christ's. That's why the mark of the Spirit's power is our commitment to the Spirit's agenda, to being, in our generation, His witnesses. For who else will be? It is our commitment to proclaiming the wonderful deeds of

God, and speaking the word of the Lord, and living the life of Christ, in the power of the Spirit, so that everyone who calls on the name of the Lord will be saved.

The Spirit-filled Christian and the Spirit-filled church will have evangelism at the top of their list. Let's not pretend that we are spiritual people, if we are not concerned about the lost people all around us. Christ redeemed us in order that the blessing given to Abraham might come to the Gentiles, so that by faith we might receive the promise of the Spirit. That's what God is concerned about. That's the fulfilment. That's why He gave the gift. So that all through the world the glory of Jesus might be revealed, and multitudes of people, from every tribe and kindred and nation might be brought into His kingdom.

If you and I this week have truly confessed our bankruptcy and cried to God for mercy, and if we've truly come to the cross as needy sinners and found forgiveness again through His grace; if we have crowned Him Lord of our lives, and we're seeking to live a life of self-emptying; and if tonight we are thanking Him because we have already received the free gift of the Spirit, and we're asking Him to flood every area of our lives—then what will be the mark of reality, next Thursday night, when you're at home?

It won't just be that you've gone back and shared with your Christian friends what a wonderful time you had. It will be that you and I will really mean business about the number one item on God's agenda: getting the gospel out into the world, starting in our Jerusalem.

When will our evangelical churches start to be really evangelistic? We prefer the comfort of our own security, because we realise that we live in a generation where many people are very far from God, and if we're really going to mean business being His witnesses it will mean all sorts of new initiatives and sacrifices.

We will never reach this generation of unchurched people if we are not prepared to make sacrifices. We'll never reach them through our standard church services or even our standard conventions. We have got to have a heart of love, and only the Holy Spirit can enable us to make the sacrifices in our churches that we need to make in order to communicate to those who are unchurched. If you add up the time that you spend in your church councils and your discussions groups, on inward-looking activities, and compare it with the amount of time and energy and money that you use in getting the gospel out into your community—I think you will find that the proportion is totally unbalanced.

This new impetus for evangelism is the mark of the Spirit's work. And if you're a Christian, the Father has freely given you His Spirit.

I want to ask you tonight: Are you giving Him the freedom to move in your life, in your church? Are you a church that exists for those who are not yet its members? Or are you so concerned about your ingrown, inward-looking activities, that you're actually quenching and grieving the Spirit, and beginning to fall apart? Are you short-circuiting that dynamic, because there are areas in your life where you are determined to exclude Him, and because your heart is divided you've got no testimony, and very little reality.

Surely not, at the end of this week? Surely we've responded to God's word?

Well then, who are the people that you are praying for to come to faith in Christ? Who are the people that you are prepared to sacrifice for in order that they might come to know the Lord Jesus? That's the mark of the power of the Holy Spirit upon us. For He is not given to provide a fragrant bubble-bath of spiritual ecstasy for us to relax in. He is given to empower us to go back into the battle, day by day, at work, at school, at university or college, at home, in your neighbourhood.

It's tough there, of course it is—we all know it—to live for Christ and the gospel. That's where the power's seen, where Christians keep on being Christians and keep on being His witnesses. And that's His activity, because that's what Jesus was like, and He wants to make you like Him. And that's His availability, because the gift of the Father is yours as a child of God. And that's the agenda.

It was ludicrous really, wasn't it? This little group of despised men and women claiming the whole pagan world for Jesus Christ. But they went out and they did it, in the power of the Spirit. And look what happened: they received the

Holy Spirit, they obeyed the Master's words—and we are the fruit of their dedication.

So—what about you?

IMPROVING YOUR SERVE

by Rev. Liam Goligher

Philippians 2:5–11

The German philosopher Schopenhauer once told a story about a pack of porcupines that gathered together for warmth one cold winter's night. But they pricked and hurt one another, so they separated. But it was cold, so they began to snuggle up together to keep warm. But they pricked and hurt one another, so they separated. But it was cold, so they began to snuggle up together to keep warm ... and so the story goes on for another twenty minutes ...

Schopenhauer intended his story as a parable of the human race. We could say it's a parable of the Christian church, its denominationalism and also its individualism, as so often we draw together for fellowship only to separate as we hurt and grieve and injure one another in various ways.

Now one of the things the apostle Paul has been speaking about in this great letter to Philippi is the absolute primacy of the gospel of Jesus Christ. In chapter 1 he tells the Philippians that one of the things which gave great joy to his heart was their partnership in the gospel with him. And one of the things he considered absolutely vital to the advancement of the gospel was their continuing harmony. That is why he says 'Whatever happens, conduct yourself in a manner worthy of the gospel of Christ ... contending as one man for the faith of the gospel' (1:27).

But there were problems in Philippi, just as there were problems in Rome from where Paul was writing, that were

beginning to fragment that undergirding unity of the gospel
work. There was pride, among some people, and strife.
There was a reluctance to be emptied. There was an
unwillingness to be nothing. People were standing on their
dignity, refusing to stoop, refusing to take second place, to
have the servant heart. There were preachers in Rome where
Paul was who were preaching Christ 'out of envy and rivalry'
(1:15).

That is the background against which Paul is writing at the
beginning of chapter 2. This spirit of unity must be among
them, he says, if the work of the gospel is going to advance
and make progress both there in Philippi and in Rome. And
against that background Paul sets this massive theological
perspective which speaks right into the situation of pride and
disharmony that he saw in Philippi.

He points them to Christ.

The eternal Christ (2:5)

First of all, he points them to the eternal Christ–'who, being
in very nature God'. That word 'being' tells us that he was
already in existence; Jesus Christ did not begin at Bethlehem,
nor did he begin at his conception in Mary's womb. Jesus
Christ never became, Jesus Christ always was. You remember how John puts it chapter 1 of his Gospel: 'In the beginning was the Word, and the Word was with God' (1:1)–face
to face with God!–'He was with God in the beginning' (1:2),
'The world was made through Him' (1:10), and 'The Word
became flesh' (1:14). Jesus was always–what? Paul tells us:
'Who, being in very nature God'.

The language he uses here is language that denotes the
outside and the inside of something. The word used for
'nature', you'll see in the NIV footnote, includes the idea of
'form'. We sometimes use the expression about someone:
'They're in good form'. Occasionally you hear it said about a
cricketer: 'He's in good form'. It means that his performance
isn't too bad; it looks good and it seems to be effective. On
the other hand sometimes my wife will say to me 'You're in
good form today, dear', and I think that is something to do
with my inner self that day: that I am happy, relaxed, co-
operative and helpful and doing all the things that she would

like me to do. But the more usual meaning of 'form' has to do with the outside of things, their shape and structure.

So there are two meanings. And the word that Paul uses here can have both. He is saying that Jesus, however you examine Him, however you look at Him, inwardly or outwardly, is in His very nature God. You don't get greater than that!

He goes on to use a word (2:6) that is translated here 'equality'. It's a Greek word from which we get several English words such as 'isomorph' (which means 'the same form') and 'isometric' ('equal measure'). And there's one I vaguely remember from school–do you remember the isosceles triangle? You know, it's the one that had two equal sides.

Jesus is God's equal. Paul is stressing this because it relates to what was going on in Philippi. There were people who were standing on their dignity. He says: I want to speak to you about someone who *is* dignity. I want to speak to you about the Lord Jesus.

Jesus is by very nature God, He is God's equal. And that means several things. It means that in Christ you see all the attributes of God. Anything you can say about God you can say about Jesus. Speak about God's love or God's justice or God's patience or God's grace or God's kindness or God's truth or God's holiness: anything you can say about God you can say about Jesus. He has all the attributes of God. He has all the prerogatives of God.

Is God worthy of worship? Jesus is worthy of worship. Is God able to forgive sins? Jesus is able to forgive sins. He has all the attributes of God, all the prerogatives of God–and he has all the functions of God: functions like providence; even the wind and the waves obey Him. Functions like redemption; He came to save his people from their sins.

So these opening sentences point us in two directions. They make statements about Jesus, that He is God–and they make statements about God that tell us that God is Christlike. Christ is God. God is Christ-like. Christ is the very revelation of God. How does the invisible God become visible, for men to see Him? He becomes visible in Jesus. In God, Paul says, there is no un-Christlikeness at all. And–

here is a surprising thing—there is nothing in the nature or form of God that is inconsistent with self-humiliation or self-emptying. That's amazing: there is nothing in the nature or form of God that precludes him from a servant-like spirit.

Paul points us to the eternal Christ.

The emptied Christ (2:6–8)

Then, secondly, he points us to the emptied Christ, Christ emptied of His glory. Do you notice there are two movements in Christ's act of self-humiliation? First, He didn't consider equality with God something to be grasped. Then secondly, He emptied Himself; He made Himself nothing.

Remember the context: Paul is writing to this church that is torn apart. There are status seekers in Philippi. There are people there who are caught up with their place, their position, their prestige and their prominence: people clinging to their dignity. We all know how that works out in practice: we like to be recognised, we like to be given our place, we like to be consulted. Maybe you're an elder in a church, and if something happens and you haven't been consulted, you feel offended. You like to be given your place.

I remember an experience I had a number of years ago. We emigrated to Canada. I was about twenty-five at the time and I went to be the senior minister, believe it or not, in a church in Canada. They had great faith! I suppose I looked older than I was…I remember how I felt when I went to pastors' conferences and they asked me where I was from; and then they said 'And how is your youth ministry going?'. And I said 'Well, it's going fine.'

'You are the youth minister, aren't you?'

'Well—not really, I'm just the young senior minister.' I can still remember how upset I used to get if I was introduced somewhere as the youth minister, when I was the senior minister.

You see, there is in every one of us this sense of our own dignity. We stand on it, we want to be recognised. But what is our dignity, compared with the dignity of Jesus? That's the point that Paul's making to these Philippians. And yet when Jesus comes He doesn't come in all the paraphernalia or insignia of deity as He did at Sinai, or as He will at His second coming. He made Himself nothing. He literally emptied himself.

The theologians have had a great time trying to work out what He emptied Himself of, but I want you to notice that Paul's statement here is an absolute statement. He doesn't tell us what He emptied Himself of, he says He emptied Himself, and then He took. In the original the emphases fall something like this: 'Himself He emptied, taking'.

The self-emptying, the humiliation of Christ was not a humiliation of subtraction but of addition. It's what He took that is significant, as Paul describes it here. Look at the three things He takes. He took the form of a servant. There's no suggestion of His laying aside His deity, only laying aside the display of His deity, the glory of it – 'The glory I had with you before the world began' (John 17:5). In Galatians 4:4 we read that 'God sent his Son, born of a woman, born under the law': that is, he was born as one obligated to obedience.

The theologians would say that He was in a covenant-of-works relationship with God. He came to be God's servant, He came to be His people's servant. Do you remember how He drove this home in John 13 when He washed His disciples' feet? To be a servant, a slave in the ancient world was to be a dependant, one obliged to obey. As far as society was concerned it meant to be a nobody. But Jesus had to become the servant if He was to become our Saviour.

Do you remember that great language where God says through Isaiah that He's going to send His servant? It's a servant who will suffer, a servant who will be despised and rejected of men (see Isa. 52–53). Jesus had to become the servant if he was to become our Messiah and our mediator.

He took the form of a servant. He took the likeness of a man. It's the same word as is used of His deity earlier on. Both inwardly and outwardly He became a real man. He became holy man.

Now this left Him wide open to misunderstanding. What He was in His dignity was obscured. At Philippi there were people who wanted to be recognised for what they were. But how did people find Jesus? 'In human likeness'. There was nothing in His outward appearance that would point to His deity. Martin Luther speaks of the 'divine incognito'. Peter caught a glimpse of that glory when he confessed Him as the Christ at Caesaria Philippi, but Jesus told him that flesh and blood had not revealed it to him. It wasn't what he saw that had led him to that confession. It was his Father in heaven who had revealed it to him. Calvin speaks of the veiling of the identity and glory of the Saviour. When you look at Jesus the man, you find in him no obsession about being recognised. He took the form of a servant and the likeness of a man.

And he took the death of a cross.

Jesus was no passive victim: He chose the way of obedience, and was obedient right up to the point of death. He went to that point of self-denial, not because He deserved death but because that was His Father's will; it was the way of obedience. He voluntarily surrendered Himself and steadfastly throughout the course of His ministry He resisted the temptation to dodge that call to the death of the cross.

In His death His deity was even more obscured. Where were people most likely to look for God? Not on Calvary on a Roman cross. The death of the cross was the death of anathema, the cursed death. 'Cursed is everyone who is hung on a tree,' Paul wrote to the Galatians (Gal. 3:13), quoting the Old Testament (Deut. 21:23).

We have a Moslem neighbour with whom I spent a few hours recently. The great stumbling-block preventing him from accepting Christianity is the claim that Jesus died on the cross. Islam rejects this: if He was truly a great prophet God wouldn't have let Him die there, because that would have put Him under the curse. So they speak of His 'swoon' on the cross and His recovery later in the tomb.

But the New Testament teaches that He died. He gave Himself to the uttermost, to the torture of crucifixion, to the horror of sin-bearing and to God-forsakenness. On that cross the God-nature was completely obscured; the veil was drawn effectively over the God-nature of the Son of God. How effective was that obscuring? Ask those two men on the road to Emmaus: 'We thought this was He.' How effective was that curtain drawn over the God-nature of the Son of Man? Listen to Jesus Himself on the cross: in His extremity He is not even able to call God 'Abba'. We see the emptied Christ.

The exalted Christ (2:9–11)

The third image that Paul points us to in these verses is that of the exalted Christ. The word 'therefore' is a key word, for Christ's exaltation is linked to his obedience. Compare this with John 17:4–5 where Jesus speaks to His Father about the glory that He had with the Father before the creation of the world. He claims that glory. In fact He claims two things.

He says 'Father, I claim the salvation of My people on the one hand and I also claim the return to that glory I had with You before the world was. And I claim these things, both their salvation and my glory, on the basis of My finished work. I have finished the work You gave Me to do.'

So Paul gives us this great outline of the exaltation of Christ. Jesus is crowned: God has exalted Him to the highest place. Literally, God has hyper-exalted Him. He has poured all His wisdom and power and energy into preparing for Jesus a glory that is commensurate with his obedience and His achievment. God has highly exalted Him, far above all principalities and powers and things made in heaven and earth and under the earth. And the amazing thing is that Christians are to share that hyper-exaltation! Romans 8:37 says we are hyper-conquerors, through Him who loved us.

He is crowned; and he is identified, for he is given 'the name'. Every Jew would have known what that name was: the forbidden name, the name for Jehovah. In fact 2:10 is drawn from Isaiah 45:23 where Jehovah vows to make Himself the object of universal worship and adoration. Here Paul applies that verse directly to Jesus. God has exalted Him and given Him 'the name'.

Jesus is crowned, Jesus is identified–and Jesus is recognised. The day is coming when He will be given His due. And He will be recognised as the one He really is, when the obscurity of the past and the invisibility of the present will be completely removed and every eye shall see Him for what He is, in all of His glory. Believers and unbelievers alike shall recognise His identity. It is mandated that every knee should bow and every tongue confess that He is Lord. And it is on the basis of that mandate that we call on men and angels and demons to bow their knee to the Lordship of Jesus Christ.

Now you understand that it is the destiny of the Christian

one day to share in His exaltation. Is Jesus crowned? Then, James says, we shall receive the crown of life which God has promised to those who love Him (Jas. 1:12). Is Jesus identified, as the Son of God, by His resurrection from the dead? Then, says Paul, all creation is on tiptoe waiting for that day when the sons of God will be revealed (Rom. 8:19). Is Jesus recognised? Then says the apostle John, though at this moment what we will be has not yet been made known—it's hidden—we know that when He shall appear we shall be 'like Him', for we shall see Him as He is (1 John 3:2).

That's our destiny. But let not our vision of our destiny cause us to lose the vision of our present duty. For why is Paul making this statement? He is making a statement so that our attitude should be the same as that of Christ Jesus, for between this day and that day, when He shall be acknowledged and recognised as Lord, we are to have the attitude of Christ.

Let me summarise what that is. It means that we must suffer with Him if we will reign with Him. It means that we must deny ourselves if we would find ourselves. It means that we must empty ourselves if we would be filled. It means that we must humble ourselves if we would be exalted.

Let's ask ourselves: 'In the church from which I come, am I the problem, because I'm standing on my dignity, wanting always to be consulted? Do I feel aggrieved by someone who hasn't recognised what I have done or applauded my behind-the-scenes work? Is there in my heart an unwillingness to lay aside my dignity and to become the servant of God's people?'

If there is, then I don't have the attitude that was in Christ Jesus; who, being in very nature God, emptied himself.

WHO DO YOU SAY I AM?

by Rev. David Cohen

Luke 9:18–27

To Australians like me, the idea of lords and ladies belongs to a different world. We do have 'ladies', in that the wife of somebody who's been knighted automatically gains the title 'Lady', but we don't have any 'lords' like you have here. And as we talk now of Jesus as Lord and compare that lordship with that of a British aristocrat, they seem to be poles apart.

Biblical doctrines such as those of Jesus as lord and Jesus as head become systematised. We talk about 'lordship' and 'headship'–words which don't exist in the Greek, but which we have coined to systematise teachings of scripture.

Liam very clearly explained to us what Jesus as Lord actually means–an emptying, a denying, a humbling, a servant's spirit. And yet it seems that all too often we take the ideas and we translate and mistranslate them, creating structures and systems that are different from what Jesus came to live. And within the very church that He founded we discover hierarchies, personality cults, people-centred ministries and 'important' people. Yet the wonderful thing about 'Jesus is Lord' is that He gives us freedom, He doesn't impose His lordship on us. Lordship is His by right and by nature, but then He hands us the freedom to reject that lordship in a way that human hierarchies and systems very often don't allow, even those within the church itself.

In Luke 6:5 Jesus told His disciples, 'The Son of Man is Lord of the Sabbath.' Notice, not 'Lord of a person'. He wasn't lording it over a person, He was the Lord of the Sabbath–the whole of creation, because the Sabbath goes back to the creation principle. The world was subdued, if you like, to His lordship; but He didn't lord it over His disciples. On the contrary, He came and took the towel. And as Liam reminded us, He washed the feet of the disciples. That was the sign of His lordship.

And yet we preen ourselves in our human importance and feel we've made it when we get on and get known. Not so with Jesus. At Pentecost, Peter in that marvellous sermon where so many were converted said, 'Therefore let all Israel be assured of this: God has made this Jesus, whom you crucified, both Lord and Christ' (Acts 2:36). Again we find this mystery of Jesus as Lord, crucified as a criminal on a cross. He is the Christ of the paradox. From the beginning to the end of Jesus's life there are paradoxes. He turns our standards upside down. We think of 'Lord', we think of 'Lord of the Manor', we think of wealth, we think of fame, we think of power, we think of authority–and then Jesus comes and takes a towel, and turns all our standards completely upside down.

And yet Paul had the hope, writing to the church at Rome, 'that if you confess with your mouth, "Jesus is Lord," and believe in your heart that God raised him from the dead, you will be saved' (Rom. 10:9).

Here for Paul the mark of lordship was the risen Christ. That was the proof that Jesus was who He claimed to be, even though the image was so different to the suffering servant of the prophet Isaiah.

So with the church in Corinth that was in such a mess, just like most of our churches today. Has it ever occurred to you, by the way, that we wouldn't have most of our New Testament if the early church hadn't been in such a mess? People say 'If only we could be like the New Testament church.' But we are! That's why we need the New Testament.

Paul reminds the Corinthian church, 'Yet for us there is but one God, the Father, from whom all things came and for whom we live; and there is but one Lord, Jesus Christ, through whom all things came and for whom we live' (1 Cor. 8:6).

You have this totality bound up in Jesus. Everything makes sense in Him, despite the paradoxes, despite the way He turns the standards of the world upside down.

It was the earliest creed: 'Jesus is Lord.' What was He Lord of? He was the Lord of the church. 'God placed all things under his feet and appointed him to be head over everything for the church' (Eph. 1:22).

Liam reminded us that all too often status and prestige seep into the church, and this ought not to be. For it's not how Jesus, the head of the church, showed us how it ought to be. Where have we gone wrong? Our organisations and structures, our hierarchies and power plays and status-seeking are all so foreign to what Jesus as Lord of the church came to live and to die for.

And just as Jesus did not consider equality with God something to be grasped (Phil. 2:6), so we, as members of the body of Christ of whom Jesus is the head, should not be grasping at that lordship which is reflected in power and status and prestige; that should be no part of our thinking or our lifestyle.

And yet if there is that status-seeking and prestige-grasping in the church, let's not be too disillusioned: because it's nothing new.

The mother of Zebedee's sons was asking Jesus whether her two boys could sit one on Jesus' right hand and the other on His left, when ultimately they came into glory. Jesus said to them, 'You know that the rulers of the Gentiles lord it over them, exercising authority over them. Not so with you,' said Jesus. 'Just as the Son of Man did not come to be served, but to serve, and to give his life as a ransom for many' (Matt. 20:25–28).

Compare that with the hierarchy and power-play we see all too often in churches of any denomination and none. And those who have formed new churches to get back to the New Testament ideal all too soon set up the same sorts of structures, power-shepherding and personality-focused ministry. I believe Jesus as head of the church is saying 'This ought not to be if I am your Lord, for I gave you an example, and I have given you the resources to live out that lordship in your lives.'

But I always have to ask a simple question about that

biblical foundation Liam gave us from Philippians 2: 'So what?' What is the implication, if Jesus is head, if He is Lord? What does that mean to you and me in 1991, as we leave the paradisaical surrounding of Keswick and go back down from the mountainside on Saturday morning?

It seems to me that there are three simple answers. If Jesus is Lord then, firstly,

He is Lord of the past

Liam reminded us that He is the eternal God. The very nature of God was bound up in Jesus (Phil. 2:6). Other theologians describe it a little more complicatedly as 'the pre-existent Christ'. I don't know about you, but I find that a little difficult to take in. I believe it by faith: that Jesus always was, because He actually said as much. The Bible tells me that Jesus is the same yesterday and today and for ever. Jesus said, 'Before Abraham was born, I am' (John 8:58). The grammar doesn't make much sense, but the underlining meaning does. The pre-existent eternal Christ is the Christ, the Lord of the past. So what?

It says to me that He is the Lord of my past, and yours. Back then, when things were as I wished they had never been, Jesus was Lord and is Lord. He knows all about that and has dealt with all of it, if I've brought it all to Him and turned from it. It's been nailed with Him to the cross and is finished. And when He cried 'It is finished!' He meant it. All that needs to be done has been done, and the Lord of the past has dealt with your past and mine. Isn't that a liberating reality for us? To understand 'Jesus as Lord' as 'Lord of the past'—'Before Abraham was, I am.'

That means that even forty-nine years ago when I was born, Jesus was Lord of my life. I didn't know Him then. I came into a knowing relationship with Him later on. But way back there He was Lord—and still is, for Jesus is the same yesterday, today and for ever. What is there, my sister and my brother, in your life tonight, that you wish could be wiped out? The teaching that Jesus is Lord can deal with it.

In this tent tonight there are many scars and wounds represented which Jesus is longing to erase. The truth of the gospel of Jesus Christ is: 'Jesus is Lord of the past'. And my sin, my guilt, the hurt, the damage, have been dealt with. It's retrospective in effect. I can look back in my life to see mistakes and errors that I've made which He's redeemed, in some mysterious way sanctified and made something worthwhile of. He is the Lord of the past.

But also,

He is Lord of the present

It's sometimes very hard to see and believe that, isn't it. I suspect there are some here tonight who feel, 'Where is He? Where is the evidence that Jesus is Lord of my life at the moment, with everything falling apart?' A husband walked out, a child gone off the rails, the tragedy that you've had to face in recent days; a desperate sense of concern and burden for what life is bringing to you right now.

If Jesus is Lord, He's not only Lord of the past, but He's the Lord of today and tonight. And when He says 'I will never leave you nor forsake you,' He means it. It wasn't a light promise He made. And we can take comfort from Jesus Himself. There are those among us tonight who will be feeling in their heart, 'If only what I'm having to put up with at the moment could be taken away from me!' What did Jesus say the night before Calvary? 'Father, if only this cup could be taken from me. But not what I want, may your will be done.' Thy will be done on earth, as it is in heaven.

If Jesus is Lord of the present He is with us. He's with us in our thoughts, in what we read and what we see and what we do and where we go. Is He Lord of today, in your life and in mine? The natural response is for each of us to feel terribly guilty. 'No, I would have to change things.' And yet, the liberty that comes from knowing that God is aware of everything we do!

The old teaching was, 'Is Jesus Lord of every room of your life?' I remember being told many times in my teens: if Jesus is not Lord of all, then Jesus is not Lord at all. And you have this awful burden of guilt, knowing full well that there are parts of our lives over which Jesus isn't currently Lord. But the Lord of the present says, 'I know you, I know everything there is to know about you. And I love you, I want you to be My friend.' That's why He said, 'I'm your friend if you do what I tell you' (see John 15:14). He doesn't want to call us slaves and servants, Jesus said: He wants to call us friends, and brothers and sisters. What higher dignity is there for us, than to acknowledge Jesus is Lord and to accept Him as a friend who already knows all there is to know about us?

One of the most radical break-throughs in my ministry was when somebody told me that Jesus cannot love me or you any more than He does right now. Let that sink in: Jesus cannot love you any more than He does right now, because He loves you totally and fully, so much so that even if you had been the last person in this world He would have given His life for you.

That's what the world needs to hear. That's what the lordship of Jesus means, a lordship expressed in love, a love that (Liam reminded us from Philippians 2) didn't grasp at equality with God. He emptied Himself to be our servants, so that we in turn, acknowledging His lordship, might serve one another, and not pushing for power and prestige and status. May it disappear from the church of Jesus Christ and from the platform of Keswick!

He is Lord of the past, He is also the Lord of the present. And of course,

He is Lord of the future

Liam spoke of destiny and duty. If Jesus is the Lord of my future, then I can comfortably leave my future in His hands, without plotting, planning or any anxiety about what might happen. Remember the old cliché 'I don't know what the future holds, but I do know who holds the future.'

Paul said to the church at Philippi that one day every tongue will confess that Jesus Christ is Lord (see Phil. 2:11). That day is surely coming. And the whole world is going to acknowledge the lordship of Jesus Christ.

In Luke 9–again, Liam referred to this–Jesus was praying privately. His disciples were with Him and He asked them, ' "Who do the crowds say that I am?" They replied, "Some say John the Baptist; others say Elijah; and still others, that one of the prophets of long ago has come back to life." ' You see, there was prestige, status, prominence, position and power if Jesus in fact was Elijah or John the Baptist or one of the prophets from long ago. But Jesus disclaimed all that. He was actually something more, but He disclaimed even that. ' "But what about you?" he asked. "Who do you say that I am?" Peter answered, "The Christ of God." Jesus strictly warned them not to tell anyone. And he said, "The Son of Man must suffer many things and be rejected by the elders, chief priests and teachers of the law, and he must be killed and on the third day be raised to life." '

Isn't it sad? It was the religious people themselves who rejected Jesus and killed Him. And is it not too far from the truth to say that the same is happening today? That those of us, the religious, are in danger of doing exactly the same as the elders, the chief priests and the others did? The teachers of the law? 'Then Jesus said to them all,' which I believe includes you and me, ' "If anyone come after me, he must deny himself and take up his cross daily and follow me. For whoever wants to save his life will lose it, but whoever loses his life for me will save it. What good is it for a man to gain the whole world, and yet lose or forfeit his very self?" '

My future is in the hands of Jesus who is Lord, for Jesus is the same yesterday, today and forever. 'Before Abraham was born, I am,' said Jesus. Jesus, if He is Lord, is Lord of the past, your past, your sin, your guilt, your shame, your unfulfilled ambitions, your broken dreams. Jesus is Lord of the past.

He is also Lord of the present. And in the midst of that mystery of suffering and pain, this call of Jesus to take up our cross daily and follow Him begins to make sense. Jesus is Lord of the present and identifies and empathises when the going gets tough–as it surely does.

But praise be, Jesus is also the Lord of the future. So all fear, all anxiety can disappear and dissolve in the absolute confidence and trust and hope (in the New Testament sense) that indeed Jesus is Lord. But that brings it back to you and to me. For just as Jesus said to His disciples when they asked Him, 'Who do you say that I am?', what about you?

Our response today is going to make a radical difference to how we live our lives: whether we will be freed from all the pressures and claims of the world, from pushing for status and prestige and power outside the church and within it. It will free us to be reflectors of Jesus, who came not to be served, but to serve, and who gave His life as a ransom for many. 'What about you?' He asks us tonight. 'Who do you say that I am?'